Last Hired,
First Fired

Last Hired, First Fired

Women and the Canadian Work Force

by
Patricia Connelly

Introduction by Margaret Benston

Copyright © 1978 Patricia Connelly
Introduction Copyright © 1978 Margaret Benston
Cover design by Liz Martin
Typesetting and Layout by Dumont Press Graphix, Kitchener, Ontario
Printed and bound in Canada

Published by The Women's Press, 280 Bloor St. W., Toronto, Ontario

Canadian Cataloguing in Publication Data

Connelly, Patricia.
  Last Hired, first fired

Bibliography: p.
ISBN 0-88961-044-4 pa.

1. Women — Employment — Canada. 2. Discrimination in employment — Canada. 3. Sex discrimination against women — Canada. I. Title.

HD6099.C65   331.4'0971   C78-001463-4

Contents

Acknowledgements

To these and all of the others who have given me help in one way or another, my sincerest thanks:

Lorna Marsden, Herb Gamberg, and Henry Beltmeyer for helping me think through some of these ideas, and Tom Cori, whose advice in the early stages was much appreciated.

Olive Ross and Debbie Josey for their superior typing effort.

The women at the Women's Press, especially Brenda Roman and Bonnie Fox for their excellent editorial work.

My parents for teaching me to work and my own family, Ralph, Kerri and Kevin, for their help and moral support.

Introduction
by Margaret Benston

An understanding of the functioning of women in the economy and in the society as a whole is of increasing importance. The question is not only one of urgency for those in the women's movement but is central to any general analysis of the economy.

The presence of women wage workers cannot be ignored. Their numbers have risen steadily since the beginning of the century, to the point where nearly 40% of the wage labour force is female. Even more significantly, married women have been entering wage labour in increasing numbers since the Second World War. Today, well over half of all women who work outside the home are married.

Women as wage workers constitute a special grouping within the labour force. Female and male wage earners differ as wage workers because women work in two places — in the home as well as in the office or factory. These apparently distinct spheres of work are both parts of the same economic whole, and a historical materialist approach must take both into account. Traditional Marxist analyses, however, have tended to concentrate on only one of these — the area of commodity production. The work done in the last few years by feminist Marxists such as Patricia Connelly has shown that not only is non-commodity production in the home a crucial part of a capitalist economy but that the *connections* between work in the home and work in commodity production are equally central.

Because of their responsibility for work in the home,

women are vulnerable to exploitation as wage workers. Certain aspects of this vulnerability — low wages, the experience of discrimination in hiring and promotion, difficulty in unionizing — have been extensively documented. This same vulnerability to exploitation leads also to women's role as a reserve army of labour, an aspect of women's situation that has been studied less.

It is in the examination of the factors which lead women into wage work that *Last Hired, First Fired* fills a real need. By rejecting the approach that centres on subjective conditions and individual choices to explain behavior and by concentrating instead on the structural and institutional factors, Connelly provides a foundation from which to build our analysis.

Such an analysis must be historical. Knowledge that the changes in women's relationship to wage work have followed the needs of changing capitalist economies makes the individual choice model completely untenable. In the early period of industrial capitalism in England, when labour was greatly needed, women and children were drawn into wage labour in large numbers. Many married women, driven by economic necessity, worked outside the home. Poverty and long working hours ensured that most women would do little housework in the home and, indeed, family life itself was minimal. Reformers and revolutionaries of the time, Marx and Engels among them, predicted the end of traditional family life among the proletariat. It seemed that all family members, male and female, young and old, would gradually be drawn into the market as all production was moved out of the household and into the capitalist sphere. This spectre was of grave concern to such social theorists.

As we know, that did not happen. The needs of the economy changed; total wealth increased so substantially that working men could demand and win a family wage. By the second half of the nineteenth century, the ideal of the modern housewife had emerged. Women were to stop working — at least for wages. They were to withdraw from the factories and shops into their homes, there to raise children and devote their time to producing goods and services for their families. Single women were to work only until they married. The economic factors that made this possible are complex, but it is clear, particularly in studying the agitation for factory reform in England, that a large element of conscious social manipulation was required to make this new ideology acceptable.

The wealth of Imperial England underwrote the cost of this ideology in Britain. In North America, where capitalism began at a later stage, differing social conditions led to essentially the same result: married women remained out of the wage labour force until well into this century. Married women *did* work in Canada and the U.S. but they did piecework in their homes, took in boarders, or were partners in the family farm. For them, the contradiction between the work that they did and the ideal of the housewife was minimal. On this continent, it was during this present century — beginning in the twenties in the U.S. and the forties in Canada — that the large-scale movement of married women into work outside the home began.

The notion of woman-as-housewife has enormous importance in regulating women's relationship to the wage labour sphere. Women work outside the home, often reluctantly on a part-time or temporary basis, because they must. The entry of married women into wage work is facilitated by the capitalists because it is profitable. The interplay between the need for labour power and the economic conditions which impel women to fill that role is a process basic to our understanding of Canadian society. *Last Hired, First Fired* addresses these fundamental questions.

There are conflicts between work in the home and wage work, both in practical and ideological terms. Practically, there seems to be little change in the division of labour inside the home — although the wife may work for wages, she still must do the housework. There is little evidence that joint responsibility for bringing cash into the family is accompanied by joint responsibility for housework. In terms of ideological conflict, the attitudes congruent with housework — cooperation, nurturance, self-sacrifice — are scarcely compatible with those generally fostered by wage work —

aggressiveness, defence of one's own interests, and competitiveness. These conflicts, which raise fundamental questions about women's relationship to society, lead us to ask: To what extent are contradictions between work in the home and wage work undermining an ideology that is a fundamental prop for the capitalist system?

Another powerful tool that can be used to encourage or discourage the flow of women into wage labour is day care. The provision of day care in urban centres during the Second World War is the most obvious example of its use to encourage women to work. As the economic situation in Canada and the United States deteriorates, there are indications that cutbacks in day care may be used to make it harder for married women to work. This is an area that clearly requires further study. The role of private enterprise in day care, for example, is not well understood; nor is the long-term effect of socializing one of the crucial responsibilities of women.

Answers to these and related questions are tasks for the future. Such answers will require time and effort but they will certainly be based, at least in part, on the fundamental analysis offered by Patricia Connelly's path-breaking work.

Chapter 1

Women's Work

One of the most remarkable changes in the Canadian economy has been the increase in the number of women entering the labour force. As in many other countries, there has been a steady increase since the turn of the century. In recent years the largest increase has taken place among married women (see table 1.1 in Appendix B).

With more and more women entering the labour force, attention has focussed on understanding the difficulties working women face. Much has been written recently on sex discrimination in the work place. Women get paid less than men, have less than an equal chance for promotion, receive fewer fringe benefits, and are segregated into certain occupations that, for the most part, are low paying. As the *Report* of the Royal Commission on the Status of Women states, "Women generally work in a few occupations labelled 'female,' earn less money than men and rarely reach the top."[1]

While the average male has only one job, married women who work outside the home have on the average two jobs since they continue to bear the responsibility for the children and the household. Very little has been done in the way of instituting adequate day-care facilities to lessen the burden. Considering the adverse conditions under which women work, the question arises as to why married women continue to enter the work world outside the home in ever increasing numbers.

To date, most of the research dealing with the increasing work rate of Canadian women has been done within a framework of traditional economics and has described this phenomenon instead of explaining it. The traditional economists in Canada, in their attempts to explain the labour force participation of married women, employ a consumer choice model that focusses on the factors influencing a woman's decision to enter or leave the labour force.

Women, according to this perspective, "are free to choose among many different types of activity: paid employment, leisure, volunteer work, work in the home."[2] The major point of the consumer choice approach is that married women make a conscious choice to enter the labour force or not and this choice is determined mainly by subjective conditions over which they have some control. Sylvia Ostry says:

> It is true that this freedom is not boundless: at different stages of a woman's life it is closely circumscribed by family responsibilities; at different periods in the life of the community it has been severely limited by prevailing mores and social attitudes. None the less, the element of choice in the labour market behaviour of women in our culture is significant and it is this element which accounts for the characteristic variability — over time and space — of female labour force activity.[3]

In other words, a woman's decision depends on how she and others define her situation, that is, how her role is perceived on the basis of shared expectations. Research done from this perspective is concerned with identifying which women choose to work and which factors influence their personal choice.

An alternative and, it is suggested here, a more adequate way of viewing female labour force participation is to consider women as a *reserve army of labour*.[4] This view distinguishes women as members of a special group and indicates how this group provides support for other social structures. From this perspective we are able to analyse female labour force participation in terms of objective or class conditions rather than subjective or personal choice.[5] Moreover, it emphasizes women's permanent connection to the production process. It provides a link between their labour force participation and their work in the home.

How do conditions structure women's labour force participation in Canada? My approach to this problem is shaped by questions that traditional studies have either left unanswered or have not even raised. The perspective I use is consistent with a radical economic framework which has been emerging in the past few years. The theoretical and methodological basis of this radical approach is Marxism, moulded and recast in response to modern social and historical developments.[6]

MARXISM

Marx's scientific approach is premised on the assumption that every society must produce the means of its social existence, that is, must have a *mode of production*; to each mode of production correspond both a system of social relations and forms of consciousness. With reference to these basic premises, Marx formulates and adopts the materialist principle of historical explanation: the conditions of social existence are not determined by consciousness but, on the contrary, forms of consciousness are determined by these conditions.

On the basis of this principle, Marx explains the patterns of social behaviour not in terms of subjective consciousness, that is, on the basis of the meanings that people assign to their actions, but in terms of social relations that are determined (and thus explained) by the material conditions of the dominant mode of production. Marx states with respect to change in society:

> Just as our opinion of an individual is not based on what he thinks of himself, so can we not judge of such a period of transformation by its own consciousness, on the contrary, this consciousness must rather be explained from the contradictions of material life, from the existing conflict between the social forces of production and the relations of production.[7]

On this basis, it is not a question of conscious decision but of a *structure of objective conditions* of which people may or may not be aware, but over which they have little conscious control — as individuals. As Marx puts it, "It is not the consciousness of men that determines their existence, but on the contrary, their social existence determines their consciousness."[8]

These conditions under which people live and work are *class conditions*. The concept of *class*, together with all of Marx's other explanatory concepts, designates a *structure* which is visible only in its effects. In short, Marx's method is based on a *structural class analysis*.[9]

My approach centres on Marx's concept of a reserve army defined within the framework of a theory of capitalist development, as applied to conditions in Canada. Since Marx did not apply the concept of reserve army to women, I will have to both extend his use of the concept and expand its meaning (see chapter 3).

In a capitalist society the accumulation of capital creates a reserve army of labour that is available for use as capital expands. In the process of capitalist development in Canada changes have occurred in the industrial and occupational structures which have created a demand for female labour.

At the same time this process has been transforming household production by extending the market economy to encompass much of the work that women once did in the home. As household goods and services become part of the market exchange of commodities, traditional ways of doing things are made obsolete and the new goods and services become indispensable for the average standard of living. To afford them, a necessity in order to maintain an average way of life, women are forced into wage labour. As well as compelling women to leave the home, the availability of these household goods and services "frees" them from a certain amount of domestic labour and makes it possible for them to leave the home.

If women are to be considered part of the reserve army, certain preconditions and conditions must be satisfied. The preconditions are that female labour be available and cheap. The principal condition is that women compete for existing jobs.

Female labour in Canada satisfies the two preconditions of availability and cheapness. It does not satisfy the principal condition of competition for a wide range of existing jobs.

The conclusion could be drawn, then, that women do not strictly compose a reserve army. However, this conclusion is based on the assumption of one major labour market. If, on the other hand, there are two major labour markets based on sex, the principal condition would be satisfied by the competition of females for female jobs. Women would be reserve labour for female occupations. I will argue that females do indeed compose a reserve army of labour in Canada; furthermore, that although women do not in individual terms compete for men's jobs, the existence of a female labour market and the presence of women as reserve labour have an important overall effect on the male labour market and the total labour force in Canada.

Before proceeding it is necessary to inform the reader of a major difficulty in looking at women workers in Canada within a historical framework. Very little has been written on the history of working women in Canada. Researchers in other countries have at least a few important works to draw upon. For example, Alice Clark and Ivy Pinchbeck examined the lives of working women in Great Britain.[10] In the United States Alice Henry and Edith Abbott investigated the conditions of industrial workers and trade union women.[11] Canadian writers, however, did not produce any works comparable to these.

The writing of women's history is just beginning in this country. A recent significant contribution is *Women at Work*, a collection of essays dealing with various forms of women's work during the period of industrialization in Canada.[12] These histories and the few others that exist provide important sources of data for this study. However, much remains to be done in this area. Indeed, most questions regarding the history of women have not yet been asked, let alone answered. In the absence of these histories, I have only the option of using official sources of historical statistics and reinterpreting them in my framework of analysis.

Chapter 2

Reserve Labour in a Capitalist System

To understand how women function as a labour reserve it is first necessary to understand how capitalism creates an industrial reserve army of labour.[1]

Capitalism is a mode of production in which (1) the worker's capacity to work, known as *labour power*, becomes a *commodity*, that is, an object which is bought and sold, and (2) the capitalist's purchase of a worker's labour power for the period of a working day is the dominant form of production.

In explaining the development of capitalism, Marx began with an analysis of *simple commodity production*, that is, a society in which producers owned their own *means of production*. When individual producers owned and worked with their own tools, they were able to sell what they produced to buy other products which they used to satisfy their needs. They started with the commodities they produced, turned them into money, and then once again into commodities for their own use (Commodities — Money — Commodities). For example, farmers sold their products for money to buy the goods they needed but were unable to produce for themselves. However, when people left farms for the city, they no longer had farm products to sell. They had only their own ability to work.

The main difference between simple commodity production and capitalism is that under capitalism the means of production no longer belong to individual producers but rather to the capitalist. The only way workers can meet their needs is to sell their labour power, their capacity to work. Labour power under capitalism becomes a commodity which is exchanged for what the workers need in order to subsist.

The capitalist[2] goes to market with money and buys certain commodities, namely, means of production and labour power. The labour power working on the means of production creates a product which the capitalist brings back to the market and converts into money (Money — Commodities — Money). However, at the end of this process the capitalist has more money or capital than when he started (Money — Commodities — Money *plus*). With this larger amount of capital he is able to buy more labour power and more of the means of production and therefore make more money which he in turn converts into additional capital, and so on. This is the process of *capital accumulation*.

To grasp Marx's conception of the reserve army it is necessary to understand its relation to this accumulation process. Capital accumulation, the driving force of capitalist development, is related to the reserve army in two fundamental ways. A reserve army of labour is both created by, and is a necessary condition of, the process of capital accumulation. We will first consider how the reserve army is created by the expansion of capital.

THE EXPANSION OF CAPITAL AND THE CREATION OF THE RESERVE ARMY

As we have seen, at the end of the exchange process under capitalism the capitalist ends up with more money than he begins with. Let us examine how that can be. In simple commodity production, workers with their own tools worked long enough to produce the number of commodities which, when sold, could buy what they needed to subsist. When it became necessary for labourers to sell their labour power to the capitalist, however, the capitalist was able to take advantage of the unique quality of labour power to produce his profit.

12

Just as they did for themselves in simple commodity production, workers under capitalism produced for the capitalist a value equal to what they needed to maintain and reproduce themselves. Marx called this *necessary labour*:

> If the value of those necessaries represent on an average the expenditures of six hours' labour, the workman must on an average work for six hours to produce that value.
>
> That portion of the working-day, then, during which this reproduction takes place, I call *"necessary"* labour-time, and the labour expended during that time I call *"necessary"* labour.[3]

The unique quality of labour power as a commodity, however, is that it is able to produce *more* value than is necessary to reproduce itself. Workers are able to work past necessary labour time and are contracted to the capitalist to do so. The time worked beyond that needed to produce the value necessary for the worker to live and continue to work is called *surplus labour*.

> During the second period of the labour-process, that in which his labour is no longer necessary labour, the workman, it is true, labours, expends labour-power; but his labour, being no longer necessary labour, he creates no value for himself. He creates surplus-value which, for the capitalist, has all the charms of a creation out of nothing. This portion of the working-day, I name surplus labour-time, and to the labour expended during that time, I give the name of surplus-labour.[4]

When sold, the product of surplus labour becomes *surplus value* — the source of profit for the capitalist (chart 2.1).

Surplus value is converted into additional capital in the accumulation process. Since the aim of the capitalist is to expand his capital, his main interest is in increasing surplus value. To do this he must increase the amount of the surplus labour extracted from the workers. According to Marx there are two methods for increasing surplus labour: the production of *absolute surplus value* and the production of *relative surplus value*.

> The production of absolute surplus-value turns exclusively upon the length of the working-day; the production of relative surplus-value, revolutionises out and out the technical

CHART 2.1
Surplus Labour

If Necessary Labour	=	4 Hours
& The Average Day	=	8 Hours

Necessary Labour	4 Hours	(Time needed to produce value necessary for maintenance of the worker)
Surplus Labour	4 Hours	(Time used to produce surplus value — the source of profit for the capitalist)
Average Working Day	8 Hours	(Amount of time for which the capitalist buys the labour power of the worker)

processes of labour, and the composition of society.[5]

During the early stages of industrialization the realization of *absolute surplus* was the aim of capital. Procuring this absolute surplus involved prolonging the working day, not just beyond the necessary labour time, but beyond the limits of human endurance. This situation eventually led to exhaustion, disease, and early death for workers, which in turn resulted in a decrease in the number of workers available. This decrease was accompanied by a corresponding rise in wages, and so, with time, the capitalist found it in his interest to limit the working day to that which could be endured (chart 2.2).[6]

CHART 2.2
Early Capitalism — Emphasis on Absolute Surplus

If Necessary Labour = 4 Hours
& Average Working Day is from 10-14 Hours

Necessary Labour	4 Hours
Surplus Labour	6 or 8 or 10 Hours
Average Working Day	10 or 12 or 14 Hours

At a later stage surplus accumulation took the form of *relative surplus*, the extraction of more surplus labour within a fixed number of hours. Workers could create relative surplus only through the use of modern machinery. Machinery made it possible for workers to produce the value necessary to sustain themselves in less time and thereby increase the surplus labour they provide for the capitalist (chart 2.3). Thus labour productivity rises, surplus value increases, and capital accumulates in modern capitalist societies.

CHART 2.3
**Advanced Capitalism — Emphasis on
Relative Surplus**

If Necessary Labour = 2 Hours
& Average Working Day is 8 Hours

Necessary Labour	=	2 Hours
Surplus Labour	=	6 Hours
Average Working Day	=	8 Hours

At first glance this process of accumulation appears to be only a quantitive change; that is, capital grows larger. However, what is actually happening is a progressive qualitative change in the composition of capital (the proportion of machinery to labour).[7] This has major consequences for those who sell their labour power as well as for the capitalist system itself.

As labour becomes more productive through the division of labour and the use of more and better machinery, the ratio of machinery to labour changes. For example, whereas at one point ten workers were needed to work ten machines, as labour becomes more productive a lesser amount of labour power is needed to work a greater number of machines (chart 2.4).

As capital grows, the labour power needed increases but in diminishing proportion, thus creating a surplus population of labourers. Marx says:

It is capitalistic accumulation itself that constantly produces, and produces in the direct ratio of its own energy and extent, a relatively redundant population of labourers, i.e., a population of greater extent than suffices for the average needs of the self-expansion of capital, and therefore a surplus-population.[8]

This surplus population is what Marx called the *industrial reserve army of labour*.

CHART 2.4
Ratio of Machinery to Labour

Originally

Amount of Means of Production	Amount of Labour Needed
Ten Machines	Ten Workers

With Higher Productivity and More Machines

Amount of Means of Production	Amount of Labour Needed
Twenty Machines	Fifteen Workers

THE RESERVE ARMY AS A CONDITION FOR THE EXPANSION OF CAPITAL

The reserve army is not simply a product of the accumulation process; it is also a necessary condition for accumulation to occur. As Marx expresses it:

If a surplus labouring population is a necessary product of accumulation or of the development of wealth on a capitalist basis, this surplus-population becomes, conversely, the lever of capitalistic accumulation, nay, a condition of existence of the capitalist mode of production.[9]

To make this clear let us consider what would happen to the accumulation process if the surplus population or reserve army of labour did not exist.

The aim of the capitalist is to expand his capital. He does this, as we have already seen, by introducing new machinery which, along with the division of labour itself and the increased productivity of labour that accompanies it, provides the power to expand capital. Capital, however, expands at an uneven pace. The capitalist must always be prepared to move into new areas of production as the opportunity develops. To do this he needs to have available a large mass of working people that can be drawn into expanding areas without damaging other spheres of production.

> [As capital expands, it]... thrusts itself frantically into old branches of production, whose market suddenly expands, or into newly formed branches, such as railways, etc., the need for which grows out of the development of the old ones. In all such cases, there must be the possibility of throwing great masses of men suddenly on the decisive points without injury to the scale of production in other spheres.[10]

A period of expansion, then, requires a sudden increase in the number of labourers; that is, it creates a demand for labour.

When the demand for any commodity increases, its price also increases. This means that its price is no longer the same as its value. In the case of ordinary commodities such as cotton cloth, certain forces are set in motion to bring prices back into line with value. Those who are producing the cloth that is in high demand, for example, start to make abnormally high profits. Then other capitalists move into the cotton cloth industry. With the eventual glut of cotton cloth on the market, the price drops until it is once again equal to the value of the cloth, and profits become normal.

Labour power, however, is not an ordinary commodity. When the demand for labour power increases there are no capitalists who can go into the production of labour power. The equilibrating mechanism of supply and demand does not operate in the case of labour power. Without some mechanism to regulate it, however, the price of labour power (wages), would continue to rise until it reached the value of the product being produced. This occurrence, of course, would eliminate the surplus value and profit which are essential to the existence of capitalism.

Since surplus value has not disappeared, and capital continues to expand, there must be some mechanism regulating the supply and demand of labour power. Classical economists accounted for the supply and demand of labour in terms of a theory of population. They argued that as capital accumulates there is a demand for labour which cannot be fulfilled, and therefore wages rise. As a result of high wages, the working population multiplies until the supply of labourers is too great. This in turn causes wages to drop and the reverse situation to occur. That is, the working population, as a result of poverty and starvation, decreases until the supply is again less than the demand, and so on.

Marx did not accept this theory. As Paul Sweezy points out, he was aware of the tendency for wages to rise under the impact of capital accumulation. He was also quite certain that wages would never rise to the point where the capitalist system would be threatened.[11] However, he disputed the theory that wages were determined by changes in population. For Marx, it is capital and not variations in the population that determines the demand and supply of labour and therefore wages. According to Marx, the mechanism for regulating the wage level and maintaining profits is contained within the capitalist system itself. This mechanism is the industrial reserve army of labour, unemployed workers who keep the wage level down by competing in the labour market.

> The industrial reserve army, during the periods of stagnation and average prosperity, weighs down the active labour-army; during the periods of overproduction and paroxysm, it holds its pretensions in check. *Relative surplus-population is therefore the pivot upon which the law of demand and supply of labour works.* It confines the field of action of this law within the limits absolutely convenient to the activity of exploitation and to the domination of capital.[12]

Population size can, of course, affect the size of the reserve army. For example, when "the expenditures of the capitalist on machinery and raw materials [grow] at the expense of labour, . . . the demand for labour lags behind the growth of total capital."[13] If the population is growing, it is logical that the reserve army will steadily expand and that the relationship between the reserve army and the total work force will remain more or less the same. Marx thought that this was likely to happen. Nevertheless, he believed that the principle of the reserve army did not depend on population growth. In fact, the reserve army is the result of capital accumulation, and it is only because of the continued existence of the reserve army that the capitalist system and the surplus value upon which it depends is able to survive.

To sum up then, the demand for labour does not increase at the same rate as the growth of capital, nor does the supply of labour available to capital increase according to the growth of the population. Since the rate of accumulation does not proceed at an even pace, capital expands in spurts rather than evenly. In an "average" period capital grows faster than the demand for labour. Increasing numbers of workers are replaced by machinery and thrown into the surplus population (or reserve army). The competition from those in the reserve army keeps wages down and adds greater pressure to those employed to become more productive and to make fewer demands for higher wages.

In a period of expansion, when new markets or industries are opening up, the demand for labour power increases. But labour cannot be drawn from one area of production to expand another area; rather there must be a portion of the population available to be absorbed into industry in an expansionary period. The reserve army provides the needed labour. When the reserve army shrinks, wages rise, and surplus value decreases. However, as Marx points out, as soon as the reserve army decreases to the point where it begins to endanger the capitalist system, a reaction sets in: "a smaller part of revenue is capitalised, accumulation lags, and the movement of rise in wages receives a check."[14] This contraction of the economy once again replenishes the supply of surplus population, and wages begin a downward trend.

On the one hand, then, the capitalist system creates a demand for labour power and on the other hand it sets "free" a portion of the labouring force to meet this demand. Thus the reserve army of labour is both a necessary product

of the accumulation process and a necessary condition for
the existence of the capitalist system.

FORMS OF THE
RESERVE ARMY OF LABOUR

According to Marx there are three forms of the reserve
army of labour: the *floating, latent,* and *stagnant* forms. It is in
the centres of industry that the *floating* form of the reserve
army is found. The introduction of machinery and the latest
technological innovations result in the displacement of
workers. Those displaced become part of the surplus population. In England at the time that Marx wrote, the manufacturing industries preferred young male workers.

> In the automatic factories, as in all the great workshops,
> where machinery enters as a factor, or where only the mod-
> ern division of labour is carried out, large numbers of boys
> are employed up to the age of maturity. When this term is
> once reached, only a very small number continue to find
> employment in the same branches of industry, whilst the
> majority are regularly discharged.[15]

The majority of these workers, Marx goes on to say, make up
the floating reserve army while the remainder emigrate,
following capital that has emigrated.

The *latent* form is found in agricultural areas. When
capitalist methods of production are introduced into agriculture, farm workers are displaced and no new jobs are created
in that industry for them to move into. As a result, labour
moves out of the rural areas and into the cities looking for
work.

The third form of the reserve army, the *stagnant* form, is
made up of those whose employment is "extremely irregular" or marginal. "It is characterized by maximum of
working-time, and minimum of wages."[16] Because of its irregular employment, the stagnant portion of the reserve
army

> furnishes to capital an inexhaustible reservoir of disposable
> labour-power. Its conditions of life sink below the average
> normal level of the working-class; this makes it at once the
> broad basis of special branches of capitalist exploitation.[17]

This form merges with what Marx called the "lowest sediment" of the surplus population — the paupers. Although pauperism is a product of capitalism and a necessary condition for capitalist production, it is not the capitalist who bears the burden of it.

> Pauperism is the hospital of the active labour-army and the dead weight of the industrial reserve army . . . . But capital knows how to throw [this weight] for the most part, from its own shoulders on to those of the working-class and the lower middle class.[18]

Marx's intention in distinguishing forms of the reserve army was solely to make visible the structures supporting the capitalist system that are necessary to the further development of capital. Capitalism creates the circumstances whereby parts of the labouring population must provide this support. It was not Marx's aim to describe the parts of the population that fall into each category. They differed, he thought, according to particular historical circumstances and must be empirically determined.

It is true that in his discussion Marx gives examples of some groups of people who made up the forms of the reserve army in nineteenth-century England. In doing so, however, he was simply illustrating the forms.

Under different historical conditions certain social characteristics make one group more competitive than another. Therefore, to determine the make-up of the surplus population, specific historical conditions must be examined. It is my intention to examine historical conditions in Canada to determine to what extent, if at all, women make up part of the reserve army of labour. In doing this I will first discuss the conditions and preconditions which must be met by any group considered as part of the reserve army of labour.

PRECONDITIONS AND
CONDITIONS FOR A RESERVE ARMY

With his recognition of the reserve army as the regulating

mechanism for the supply and demand of labour, Marx illuminated the fundamental nature of the relationship between the employed labour force and those not employed. Steady full employment, in Marx's view, is not possible in a capitalist system. The accumulation process requires both the unemployed and the employed to continue functioning. Without a reserve labour pool to draw on in an expansionary period, wages could rise to the point where surplus value and the capitalist system itself would be endangered.

It is the surplus population that makes the system viable. The labouring population moves between the active work force and the reserve army according to the needs of capital. If the economy is expanding rapidly, the number employed increases while the number in the reserve army decreases. If the economy is in a crisis period and is contracting, the reverse occurs; the reserve army increases and the number of those employed decreases.

In the case of a crisis period and in what Marx called an "average period," those in the reserve army compete with those working for existing jobs. Those needing work are willing to settle for lower wages. This competition prevents the employed from asking for higher wages and impels them to become more productive simply to keep their jobs. As labour becomes more productive, more workers are displaced, swelling the ranks of the reserve army and intensifying the competition.

From the foregoing discussion we see that through competition the reserve army exerts pressure on the employed labour force, so preserving the wage and profit level for the capitalist. Thus the necessary condition for a reserve army is that it compete with the actively employed workers for their jobs. Beyond the principal condition of competition there are two preconditions which must be satisfied by a reserve army. The first precondition is that of *availability*. A reserve army must be available to be drawn on when the economy is expanding. The second precondition is that of *cheapness*. A reserve army must provide cheap labour in order to act as the necessary threat to those employed when the economy is not expanding.

Once again it is necessary to point out that Marx developed his model at a very high level of abstraction. Marx believed that parts of the model would be modified as more aspects of reality are introduced.[19]

For example, at a high level of abstraction Marx focussed on the principal condition of the reserve army, which is competition. However, at a concrete level Marx recognized the role of trade unions in qualifying this competition. In fact, as an illustration of this recognition, Marx predicted that as soon as the workers learned that the more productive they were the more precarious their jobs became and that competition among them stemmed from the pressure of the reserve army, they would form trade unions to organize cooperation between the employed and the unemployed. Furthermore, Marx believed that as the trade unions exerted pressure, the capitalists would call for the state to interfere forcibly in support of the "sacred" law of supply and demand.[20]

Accordingly, then, the competitive character of the reserve army becomes modified when the concept is applied at a more concrete level. This will be demonstrated in our historical analysis of female labour in Canadian society. These alterations will emerge as we turn our attention to the key question: whether or not Canadian women meet the condition and preconditions of a reserve army of labour.

Chapter 3

Do Women Meet the Preconditions of a Reserve Labour Force?

In this chapter we shall focus on whether or not women meet the two preconditions of a reserve labour force. Are women workers available? Do they provide cheap labour?

WOMEN AS AVAILABLE LABOUR

The earlier structural conditions of Canadian society and the place of women's labour in it set the stage for later developments which have determined the contemporary structure of women's labour force participation. With reference to what he describes as the "toiler" society in early nineteenth-century Canada, Leo Johnson says, "There was little specialization, individual productivity was low, and commodity exchange was carried on primarily through debt relationships."[1] His description of toiler society in Ontario gives more specific features of this kind of system:

In this toiler society, the basic economic unit was the lower-class family engaged in autonomous production. Whether on the farm or in the workshop, every member of the family, from the small child to the elderly grandparent, laboured to contribute to the family's wealth. Although the family unit exchanged a certain amount of produce and labour for such necessary goods as iron ware, tin ware, books, clothing and, perhaps, a few luxuries such as tea, tobacco, fine cloth or alcohol, for the most part the family produced what it needed to consume.[2]

The importance of the work role of women in this type of productive unit was never in doubt. Once again Johnson explains:

> Within the toiler economic unit, the role of the woman was crucial. Not only did she labour directly, but she produced the children whose labour was absolutely necessary to the success of the unit. Within the toiler society, there was a clear division of labour between the men, on the one hand, and the women and children on the other. While the men worked in the fields or woods, or sold their labour power off the farm, the women and children worked as a production unit in the area immediately surrounding the house, garden and outbuildings.[3]

Before industrial capitalism became the dominant mode of production, all members of the family laboured together to produce those things (*use values*) necessary for their existence; while the kind of work they performed differed according to the social division of labour, the definition of their labour in relation to production was the same — they both produced use values.[4]

In the process of capital accumulation in Canada the productive conditions of the toiler society were gradually transformed, creating the basis for a new type of society — capitalist society.[5]

The capitalist system of social relations develops on the basis of conditions established in production. One of these conditions is a division of labour that not only leads to the formation of a new class division but also affects the relations between men and women.

Under capitalism the labour process assumes two new characteristics. The labouring part of the population now works under the control of the capitalist to whom their labour power belongs. In addition, the product of their labour no longer belongs to them but to the capitalist.

Once the capitalist gains control of two of the basic factors of the labour process, the raw material and the instruments or tools for production, the majority of people are unable to produce the use values necessary to meet their needs. In order to survive they are forced to sell the only thing they do own, namely, their labour power. Thus two new classes are formed, the bourgeoisie who own the means of production and the proletariat who own nothing but their labour power.

The capitalist uses the labour power that he has purchased to produce commodities. A commodity is produced for exchange rather than for the use of the producer. All commodities have use value; that is, they are capable of satisfying some need or want. However, use values are produced by the capitalist because and only insofar as they also have an *exchange value*. The capitalist gets his profit by exchanging the commodity for more money than it cost him to buy the labour power of the worker who produced the commodity, together with the raw materials and a fraction of the means of production used to make it. Commodity production reaches its greatest development under capitalism.

At the same time that it becomes necessary for some family members to sell their labour power, it is also essential that certain things with only use value continue to be produced, those things having to do with the reproduction of labour, the rearing of children, and the maintenance of the home. Because of the existing division of labour between males and females, women continue to be primarily responsible for producing these use values and men become primarily responsible for selling their labour power to the capitalist. As Eli Zaretsky states:

> . . . the overall tendency of capitalist development has been to socialize the basic processes of commodity production — to remove labor from the private efforts of individual families or villages and to centralize it in large-scale corporate units. Capitalism is the first society in history to socialize production on a large scale. With the rise of industry, capitalism "split" material production between its socialized forms (the sphere of commodity production) and the private labor performed predominantly by women within the home.[6]

With the advent of industrial capitalism, then, the general labour process was split into two separate spheres; commodity production, done mainly by men in industry, and domestic labour, done by women in the home. As the result of this separation of domestic and industrial spheres under capitalism, men's and women's labour is no longer defined, as it was in the "toiler" society, in the same way. Under capitalism men are basically defined as commodity producers; they either own or operate (as a result of selling their labour power) the means of production. On the other hand, women as a group stand in a relation to production different from that of men as a group. Margaret Benston tentatively defines women as "that group of people who are responsible for the production of simple use-values in those activities associated with the home and family."[7]

By the turn of the century in Canada, women had been essentially defined out of the capitalist labour market. Although some women have always sold their labour power to the capitalist, it was at this point that women as a group became an available source of labour power for the capitalist system. Indeed, women became an *institutionalized inactive reserve army of labour*.

WOMEN AS CHEAP LABOUR

Not only did the labour of men and women become defined differently under capitalism, female labour power also became differentially valued.[8] As we have seen, men's labour under capitalism is defined in terms of the production of commodities for a wage while women's labour is defined predominantly in terms of the production of use values in the home. Although women's domestic labour is socially necessary labour and is essential to the maintenance of the capitalist system, it is unpaid labour; that is to say, the labour power of women who work in the home has no exchange value.

Since it is men's primary responsibility to sell their labour power, it is their labour power which has both exchange value and use value. Women's domestic labour, on the other hand, has only use value. While this is the case with female domestic labour, the concern here is with the value of women's wage labour. What occurs when women sell their labour power as men do, when women produce commodities? Does the labour power of men and the labour power of women have the same value?

First we must consider how the value of labour power is determined. Marx was the first to recognize that labour power is a commodity and its value is determined in the same way as the value of other commodities. The value of labour power, like that of any commodity, is determined by the labour time necessary for the production (and in this case *re*production) of that commodity.[9] The production of labour power consists of the maintenance and reproduction of the labourer. The value of labour power is equal to the cost of its own maintenance and reproduction. Marx says:

> Labour-power exists only as a capacity, or power of the living individual. Its production consequently pre-supposes his existence. Given the individual, the production of labour-power consists in his reproduction of himself or his maintenance .... The value of labour-power is the value of the means of subsistence necessary for the maintenance of the labourer.[10]

Since according to Marx labour power which is withdrawn from the market as a result of wear and tear must be continually replaced, the means of subsistence necessary for the production of labour power must include that necessary for the labourer's children.[11] Thus the value of labour power is equal to the value of the commodities needed for the labourer's maintenance and reproduction. Marx assumes, then, for the purposes of his analysis, that labour power exchanges for its value. As Paul Sweezy states, in his discussion of Marx's analysis, " ... the capitalist buys labor power at its value, that is to say, he pays to the worker as wages a sum corresponding to the value of the worker's means of subsistence."[12]

The necessary means of subsistence are historically and culturally defined. What is needed to maintain and reproduce the worker varies according to different circumstances. However, the amount needed to subsist in any particular society at any particular time is readily known. Unlike that of other commodities, then, the determination of the value of labour power has a moral and historical element.[13]

Since labour power must be maintained and reproduced if capitalism is to continue, it would seem reasonable to expect that when men and women both produce commodities, that is, sell their labour power for wages in order to produce commodities for the capitalist, the exchange value of their labour power would be equivalent. This, in fact, is not the case. Women in general have always received lower wages than men.

Let us look at the situation in Canada to see that indeed a wage differential has existed and continues to exist. It is difficult to do a historical comparison of the wages of men and women in Canada because, for the years before 1931, data on wages by sex are not available and because in general men and women have always done different kinds of work. Ceta Ramkhalawansingh, however, succeeds in getting a sense of the discrepancy between the wages of men and women in the early 1900s in Canada by considering the different rates of pay for certain occupations and the sex composition of these occupations.

> In Toronto in 1914, a building labourer working a 44-hour week could earn $13.20 per week. An electrical worker made $17.60 per week and a bricklayer as much as $24.20 per week. These relatively high paying construction trades were for the most part closed to women, as they are today.
>
> Wages in the factory were lower, and this is where many women worked. If we look at cotton textile plants as a typical example of factory wages at the time, a man could earn as little as $11.80 per week as a mule spinner in New Brunswick, or he could earn as much as $15.00 as a loom fixer in Ontario. Women in the same plants, on the other hand, earned only $6.90 per week as ringspinners and warpers in New Brunswick. The princely sum of $9.95 per week as a warper in Quebec, was about the maximum possible wage for a female textile worker.[14]

Today there are more sources of data showing the differences between the wages of women and men, although there is still not enough information to permit a thorough comparison of female and male earners for the same or similar jobs. However, where data are available they consistently show lower average rates for women than for men.

Sylva Gelber, after taking into account such factors as seniority, part-time work, regional variations in wage levels, and the male-female mix within an industry, finds substantial differences between the earnings of women and men. For example, in managerial occupations, where women make up somewhat more than one-tenth (14.3%) of all employees, the average earnings of men are twice (107.4%) those of women; in sales occupations, where women are more than one-third (38.8%) of all employees, men earn over two and one-half times (167.9%) more than women do; in service industries, where women account for almost three-fifths (59.1%) of the total work force, men earn an average of more than twice (112.6%) as much as women; and in clerical occupations, where women are almost three-quarters of the total work force, the annual earnings of men exceed those of women by more than one-half (56.7%).[15]

On the whole, men do make higher wages than women. It could be argued that men get more money than women because they do more difficult and more important jobs. Yet we find that even when men do the same "less difficult and less important 'female' jobs," their earnings are still greater.

Once again Gelber shows that full-time, full-year male baby-sitters earned, on average, more than twice (127.5%) the employment earnings of female baby-sitters during 1970. Among professions generally considered "female," Gelber found that the average employment earnings of men librarians exceed those of women by almost one-fifth (18.6%), and male dietitians and nutritionists derive average employment earnings almost one-quarter (22.6%) greater than those of female workers.[16]

Despite legislation in Canada prohibiting different rates of pay on the basis of sex, the Royal Commission on the Status of Women in Canada continually received briefs citing different pay scales for men and women doing the same jobs.

> We were told of different pay rates for women and men in certain electrical and automotive industrial organizations and in printing shops. Briefs described different pay rates in other industries too. The reasons for the differences were hard to find. We were at a loss to understand, for example, why an experienced female fish-worker would receive $2.15 an hour while an experienced male fish-worker received $2.83 an hour. We were even more mystified when we were

told that an inexperienced male fish-worker was receiving $2.37 an hour.[17]

Several explanations have been put forth by the neoclassical economists to account for wage differentials between men and women. Three of the most prevalent models used in this tradition are the *overcrowding, human capital,* and *monopsony* models. According to the *overcrowding* and *human capital* models, women and men are not equally productive, and wage differentials reflect this quality differential. According to the *overcrowding* approach, women are potentially as productive as men but because of occupational segregation they are crowded into limited numbers of labour-intensive occupations, which accounts for their lower productivity.

According to the *human capital* view, female and male workers are not equally productive because women accumulate less human capital than men do. This is so because women have less work experience and spend proportionately fewer years in the labour force than men. In other words, when the wages of workers equal the value of their *marginal product* (defined as additional output from additional employment of labour), then wage differentials between men and women are due to their differing productivity.

The *monopsony* model focusses on monopoly power in the labour market.[18] To the degree that monopsony elements exist in the labour market, the workers will get a wage which is less than their marginal product. This will mean higher profits for the employer. Because this model emphasizes power and profit, it is an advance over other neoclassical explanations of wage differentials. According to the overcrowding and human capital models, women are less productive than men and therefore receive a lower wage. According to the monopsony model, women and men are equally productive but employers are able to pay women less under certain conditions and do so because it is profitable for them. By implication, of course, if monopsony elements did not exist women would be paid wages equal to their productivity.

The question is, Do workers' wages actually represent their marginal productivity? Marx says that workers performing socially average labour are paid not for their *labour* but for their *labour power,* that is, the capacity to labour. He explains that in a capitalist society it *appears* that workers are being paid for their labour:

> On the surface of bourgeois society the wage of the labourer appears as the price of labour, a certain quantity of money that is paid for a certain quantity of labour.[19]

But in fact, according to Marx, workers are not being paid for labour but rather for labour power, which is sold as a commodity to the capitalist.

> In order to be sold as a commodity in the market, labour must at all events exist before it is sold. But could the labourer give it an independent objective existence, he would sell a commodity and not labour.
>
> That which comes directly face to face with the possessor of money on the market, is in fact not labour, but the labourer. What the latter sells is his labour-power.[20]

Because classical political economy didn't recognize this distinction between labour and labour power, it focussed on the mechanism of supply and demand in trying to understand how the price of labour was determined. But Marx points out that on examination it becomes obvious that supply and demand explains only *fluctuations* in the price of labour and not the price itself. The question is, When supply and demand are in equilibrium (that is, supply meets demand), how is the price of labour determined?

For Marx the answer was clear. The price of labour power is determined, not by supply and demand, but by its *value,* that is, by the cost of producing and reproducing the labourer. The worker's labour power is a commodity bought by the capitalist at its value, and wages as a whole correspond to the value of the worker's means of subsistence (historically defined).

According to Marx, then, the price of labour does *not* correspond to what the worker produces, but rather to what it costs to maintain and reproduce the worker. This cost is always less than the value of the commodities that the worker actually produces. In this way the capitalist makes a profit while at the same time appearing to pay for what the labourer produces.

> The value of labour-power must always be less than the value it produces, for the capitalist always makes labour-power work longer than is necessary for the reproduction of its own value.
>   The wage-form thus extinguishes every trace of the division of the working-day into necessary labour and surplus-labour, into paid and unpaid labour. All labour appears as paid labour.[21]

Under capitalism it is assumed that the family, not the individual worker, is responsible for the maintenance and reproduction of the labour supply. The male is defined as the head of the household and the family member whose primary responsibility it is to sell his labour power. Under these conditions, the man's wage includes the means of subsistence necessary for both his own and his family's maintenance and reproduction.

From the point of view of the capitalist, then, the cost of reproducing the new labour supply need not be paid to both male and female members of the family. Thus when women sell their labour power, its value is not determined by the means of subsistence necessary for the maintenance *and* reproduction of their labour power; at most it is the means of subsistence necessary to maintain their labour power.

That was certainly the case in the late nineteenth and early twentieth centuries in Canada. Lori Rotenberg uses data from the annual report of the Ontario Bureau of Industries for the year 1889 to show that women workers without dependents were left with a surplus of $2.43 once the total cost of living had been deducted from their total yearly earnings, while women workers with dependents incurred a deficit.[22]

This situation had not changed by the second decade of the twentieth century. "In the *Labour Gazette* of June, 1913, Professor C.M. Derick of McGill University stated that the average wage of female factory workers in Canada was $216/year or $5/week. The living wage at that time was considered to be $390/year or $7.50/week."[23]

Today this situation is essentially the same. One indication of this fact comes from an interview survey carried out across Canada in 1970. It was estimated that almost two-thirds (62.9%) of all welfare recipients were women. Of these women more than two-thirds (69.2%) were widowed, separated, or divorced, and more than half (54.2%) had young children.[24] Considering the cost of working, namely, transportation, clothing expenses and day care, as well as low female wages, women who are supporting a family alone simply cannot afford to work outside the home.

As these data illustrate, women are not paid the value of their labour power, which would include the cost of its reproduction. The inclusion of women in the value of men's labour power is the explanation for the lower wages accruing to female labour power in the market. The existence of distinct female occupations maintains and reinforces this inequality. So we see that under advanced capitalist forms of production, not only does female domestic labour have no exchange value, but female wage labour receives less than its exchange value.

Chapter 4

Do Women Meet the Major Condition of a Reserve Labour Force?

The discussion thus far has shown that women meet the two preconditions of reserve labour; women provide cheap and available labour. Our attention turns now to the major condition of reserve labour, that of competition.

WOMEN AS COMPETITION IN THE LABOUR MARKET

Are women in competition for most occupations in Canada? If women are competitive with men in the labour force, we would expect to find that they are represented in a majority of jobs; that is, women would be widely distributed throughout the occupational system.[1] If most women work in areas where male and female labour is readily interchangeable, then we would say that female labour is competitive with male labour. If, on the other hand, most women are concentrated in only a few occupations, we would have to conclude that women do not compete directly with men. According to Valerie Oppenheimer, to the degree that women and men are concentrated in the same occupations, they tend to be relatively competitive with each other.

Using a statistical analysis of census data for the years 1901-1971, we can establish to what degree women are and have been evenly distributed throughout the labour force in Canada and therefore whether they are or have been directly competitive with men for jobs. "If women were randomly distributed throughout the occupational system, they would form the same proportion of workers in each occupation that they form in the labour force as a whole."[2] So if women were 30% of the labour force, they would also be 30% of each occupation. An uneven distribution would result in women forming a higher or lower proportion of the workers in some jobs. When women form a higher proportion, they are considered to be in *disproportionately female* occupations.

Our findings show that for every census from 1901 to 1971, the majority of female workers are concentrated in jobs that were disproportionately female; that is to say, in that seventy-year period women were in occupations where they formed a higher proportion of the workers in the occupation than they did in the labour force as a whole.

In 1901, for example, women made up 13% of the entire labour force. Having designated the occupations in 1901 which contained more than 13% women workers (e.g., 83.7% of all servants were women in 1901), we see that 85% of women workers were in these disproportionately female occupations. If women had been evenly distributed there would have been only 17% of the female work force in these occupations; in 1901 for every one woman expected (if women had been evenly distributed) there were five observed in the disproportionately female occupations. In every census year since 1901, at least twice as many women as expected were found in these occupations (see table 4.1 in Appendix B).[3]

Although there were many occupations which were disproportionately female, they could not all be considered "female" jobs. If women made up 13% of the labour force (as in 1901) and in any given occupation made up 20% of the workers, that particular occupation would be a disproportionately female occupation. However, since only 20% of the workers in that job were women, it would not be a "female" job. An occupation is considered "female" only if the majority of workers (50% or more) in that occupation are women.

The data reveal that quite a high percentage of women are concentrated in jobs that contain 50% or more workers who are female (see table 4.2 in Appendix B). For example, in 1931, 68% of all women workers were in "female" jobs. If women had been proportionately distributed throughout the occupational structure, these same occupations would have contained only 13% of the female labour force in that year.

During the 1901-1971 period, no less than 65% of the female labour force were in occupations where the majority of workers were women and no less than 43% were in occupations which were *70% or more* female. It appears, then, that over the seventy-year period the majority of women have been and still are in "female" occupations. ("Female" occupations are shown in tables 4.3, 4.4, and 4.5 in Appendix B.)

The data show that women and men are concentrated in different occupations. They are in fact in separate labour markets and therefore are not directly competitive with one another.[4] But if women are cheap and available labour, why aren't they directly competing with men for their jobs?

Certainly with the advent of industrial capitalism came the overt threat of competition from cheap labour in the form of women and children. Marx noted, "In so far as machinery dispenses with muscular power, it becomes a means of employing labourers of slight muscular strength, and those whose bodily development is incomplete, but whose limbs are all the more supple. The labour of women and children was therefore, the first thing sought by the capitalists who used machinery."[5]

In the nineteenth century in Canada, women and children were in the labour force and working under conditions that were far from satisfactory. Speaking of the conditions of labour in the period from 1880 to 1890 in Canada, Charles Lipton says, "With large scale capitalist production, came the discovery that the road to riches was exploitation of women and children. Three generations earlier, British capitalists had shown the way. Now, Canadian capitalists took up the torch." He goes on to say, "The mills were filled with women and children working in miserable conditions at miserable rates."[6]

Thus, with the rise of the factory system of industrial capitalism and the accompanying new way of organizing labour and new technology came the opportunity for Canadian capitalists to replace high-cost skilled labour with low-cost unskilled labour. As one such source of cheap unskilled labour, women became a competitive threat for men's jobs. However, as we have seen, by 1901 women had been segregated into "female" occupations and were essentially non-competitive with male labour. How did this come about?

LABOUR FORCE
SEGREGATION AND COMPETITION

Leo Johnson advances the view that both male workers and capitalists were instrumental in creating occupational segregation in Canada.[7] According to Johnson, the initial reaction of male workers to the employment of women (and children) was to oppose equal wages for them. This was done on the basis that women were not by nature equal to men; that is, they were physically weaker and morally more corruptible, and secondly, they did not have economic responsibilities equal to those of men. Later they changed their strategy to demanding equal pay and higher standards for women in the belief that under such conditions these "inferior" workers would be excluded from the labour market.

This did not happen. Instead, according to Johnson, employers arrived at an ingenious solution whereby they separated certain occupations, defined them as "female" and paid lower wages to the women who held the jobs. Through this means women were segregated from men in the work place and removed from direct competition for men's jobs. This satisfied male workers while still making it possible for employers to use females as a cheap source of industrial labour.

The response of male workers to the threat of competition from female workers was to try to exclude them from the labour force rather than to organize them. When it became clear that women could not be removed entirely, the attitude of male workers became ambivalent. The general attitude of male-dominated trade unions to women workers in the early part of the twentieth century is summed up by Alice Klein and Wayne Roberts.

> The view of the trade union movement towards the entrance of women into the work force was obviously one of apprehension! They feared this process because of its effects on the male work force and on the traditional role of women. They were anxious to define very clearly the limits to which women's sphere could be extended and still be compatible with their notion of femininity. Yet often the logic of their own interests pressed them to take a progressive stance on key issues of civil and industrial rights, thus causing considerable internal tension and ambivalence in their overall view of women workers.[8]

Today the situation is not greatly changed. In a study conducted for the Royal Commission on the Status of Women, Renée Geoffroy and Paule Sainte-Marie found in Quebec that the attitudes of men toward women workers were still ambivalent. On the one hand, as members of unions, men had to admit that women workers should have the same rights as men and that the union should see to it that these rights are recognized and respected. On the other hand, as men they continue to see the work world as their domain, an attitude based on a conception of the male as sole provider, according to which "a woman's place is in the home."[9]

Recognizing this ambivalence, we should not be surprised that trade unions have accomplished less for women workers than they have for men. A union brief submitted to the Royal Commission on the Status of Women says, "We believe we are in a position to state, ... that unionized women enjoy, with but one exception, the same working conditions as men: ... it has unfortunately been impossible, we must admit, to secure real implementation of the principle of equal pay for equal work in certain sectors."[10]

By restricting membership in job training programs or by acquiescing in the establishment of job categories or exclusion of part-time workers, some unions are still actively restricting the access of women to certain jobs within their jurisdictions. Unions continue such practices as asking for percentage increases in pay, which favour male workers, and subclassifying workers to exclude women from more highly paid jobs.[11]

One of the chief ways of maintaining occupational segregation and concomitant low wages for women is through the use of legislation. The Royal Commission on the Status of Women quotes a trade union brief that illustrates how an employer can use protective legislation to pay women less:

> We know of another instance where female and male employees do exactly the same job — winding coils. In this instance the female employees are paid eleven per cent less than the males. The job content is the same, but the females can only work on two shifts. Legislation protects women from having to work the midnight to morning shift. The fact that the men are required to do the job on the third shift is considered enough of a change in job content to deny equal pay under the law as it now stands.[12]

Kathleen Archibald describes how women have been discriminated against in the public service through the use of legislation.[13] The Civil Service Act of 1918 gave the Civil Service Commission the authority to limit job competition on the basis of sex and other characteristics. Only married women who were self-supporting were appointed to jobs. If a sufficient number of "qualified candidates" was not available, married women were hired on a temporary basis. A woman working in the public service who married was obliged to resign. If she wished to continue working and if the service needed her, she was rehired on a temporary basis and paid the minimum rate for her classification.

According to Archibald, during the Depression, when the number of jobs was decreasing in general, there was a greater decrease in the proportion of permanent jobs for women. During World War II, on the other hand, there was a sharp increase in both the number and percentage of women appointed to the public service. At the close of the war the restrictions on the employment of married women were reintroduced. Only under special circumstances were married women retained or hired, and even then they were limited with regard to salaries and advancement. Archibald gives the following illustration:

> For instance, married women in clerical and administrative positions were not allowed to advance beyond Clerk, Grade 3. A single woman who had advanced above this was demoted to Clerk, Grade 3, upon getting married, although her duties were seldom changed.[14]

The creation and maintenance of a segregated labour force by sex benefits both employers and, in some cases, male workers. It is important to recognize, however, that the role of male workers is secondary to that of the capitalists who show a major predisposition to divide the work force. The competition between wage workers is built into capitalism, and only in the short run does the division of male and female labour benefit the male worker. While occupational segregation prevents female workers from competing directly for individual male jobs, the existence of a distinct female labour market has a competitive effect on the male labour force in the long run.

Men must continually compete to establish or maintain certain occupations as more highly paid men's jobs. As long as more poorly paid female jobs exist, there is always the danger that male occupations will be re-evaluated on the basis of female occupations and wages. This is illustrated in the case of union workers in a carpet plant in Ontario who were bargaining for a new contract.[15] The male union members felt that to support the women (whose jobs had lower classifications) in their demands for a six-cent-an-hour increase in pay would be to jeopardize their own demands.

A female union official insisted that if the women's wages were not raised, men's wages would be affected at some point. As it happened, just before the contract was settled, this very thing occurred in a different factory belonging to the same company. The men's jobs were reclassified downward and their wages decreased. In the long run, as this case illustrates, it is not in the interest of male workers to maintain the occupational segregation and low wages of women since indirectly such segregation creates competition between female and male workers.

The discussion thus far can be summarized in this way: With the advent of industrial capitalism a split occurred between the public sphere of commodity production and the private sphere of domestic labour. Men became the commodity producers and women the domestic labourers. It was at this point that women were structurally defined out of the labour force and became available labour, indeed, became an institutionalized inactive reserve army of labour.

Although women as a group were defined out of the labour force, some women have always found it necessary to sell their labour power in the market. When women work outside the home they receive, in general, a lower wage then male workers. Wage differentials favouring men have always existed in Canada. The husband's wage has been expected to support the entire family.

From the capitalist point of view, women at most need to be paid only enough to support themselves until they marry. Once they marry, the cost of their maintenance and the cost of rearing children will be included in their husband's wage. In this way women's wage labour comes to have a lower value; it is cheap labour.

Having shown the existence of two labour markets — a female and male labour market — it becomes clear that direct competition between women and men for jobs does not occur. However, within the female labour market women do look for the same work and thus compete with other women for jobs. Furthermore, the existence of a separate female labour market appears to have an indirect competitive effect on male labour.

According to this argument, then, women's labour does meet the two preconditions of cheapness and availability and the major condition of competition; consequently women must be considered a reserve army of labour. We now turn to the historical forms of this reserve army in Canada.

FORMS OF FEMALE
RESERVE LABOUR IN CANADA

There have always been some women who have needed to sell their labour power. Self-supporting women, women who

were single, widowed, or separated, and women whose husbands were unemployed or underemployed have always
sought jobs outside the home. Of these women those who
were unable to find permanent work became part of the
active reserve army, specifically the floating and stagnant
forms of the reserve.

The floating form of reserve, it may be recalled from
chapter 2, includes workers who move from job to job (those
who are hired and discarded according to the movements of
capital). These workers move in and out of the reserve army
and employment. Today we can understand how women are
part of this form by considering some of the characteristics
of "female" occupations.

Along with having lower wages, the "female" occupations
generally have fewer fringe benefits and fewer opportunities for advancement. The occupations are such that,
once trained, women can move in and out of them relatively
easily. For example, clerical work, retail sales, and even the
"female" professions of teaching and nursing require little
"on-the-job" training. As an indication of this fact, there are
"floating" nurses, "substitute" teachers, and secretarial
"pools," which involve individuals moving in and out of areas
within their respective organizations as needed. For the most
part, these occupations are such that they provide *horizontal*
rather than *vertical* career patterns for women; that is,
women continue to teach, nurse, and type, with increases in
pay but not promotions. As Morley Gunderson states:

> Many of the predominantly female occupations have been
> characterized as dead-end jobs; they are not conducive to
> career advancement or to independent decision-making, and
> few are stepping-stones to more challenging jobs. In addi-
> tion, many jobs, such as cooking, cleaning, or taking care of
> children, are extensions of household activities.[16]

In such circumstances women are likely to move or be moved
in and out of "female" occupations rather easily, thus being
employed sometimes and making up part of the floating
reserve at other times.

The stagnant form of the reserve consists of those whose
employment is irregular, marginal, and casual. The applica-
bility of this form to Canadian women is readily discernible.

The number of women employed part-time is and has always been larger than that of men, and it is rising steadily. "According to the Dominion Bureau of Statistics, 22 per cent of the 2.3 million women employed in 1967 usually worked less than full time, compared to 17.3 per cent of the 1.6 million employed in 1961."[17]

The stagnant form of the reserve army also includes an even lower stratum composed of those Marx called "paupers" but today would be called welfare recipients. To a large extent women supporting children make up those receiving welfare. The costs of working, that is, day care, travel, clothes, etc., are often greater than what they can earn. However, if needed by the capitalists, these women can be drawn into the labour force if they are simply provided with free day care or other aid as was done during the war.[18] In this regard the Ontario government has put out a pamphlet for welfare mothers entitled *It Pays to Work*. It states:

> Recently . . . more and more women have been working part-time, or full-time to help support their families, maintain their job skills, and meet new people. Many Family Benefits mothers share these goals and have requested that changes be made in the Family Benefits program to assist them in moving into the labour force.
>
> In response to these requests, the program has been changed to provide greater incentives to mothers who wish to increase their income by working part-time, or eventually, full-time.[19]

Historically in Canada most women with employed husbands have not been actively employed or actively looking for employment. Prior to World War II it was unusual in Canada for a married woman to be hired or to remain on the job after marriage.[20] Having initially been defined out of the capitalist labour market, married women until relatively recently have remained out, except during the world wars. This large section of women became what I refer to as an *institutionalized inactive reserve army*.

This concept indicates that whereas men who are not part of the work force are automatically part of the active reserve army because they are defined as commodity producers, housewives constitute a different form and have a different starting point with regard to the reserve army.

The *institutionalized inactive reserve army*, however, does have a similarity to Marx's third form of surplus population, the latent form. As capitalism develops, it both contracts the basis for agricultural labour, (thereby creating a latent surplus population in the *primary*, or resource-extracting, sector of the economy), and creates a need for that labour in the *secondary*, or goods-producing sector. Likewise, as capitalism matures, it both contracts to some extent the basis for household labour (creating a latent surplus population which I have defined as an institutionalized inactive reserve), and creates a need for that labour in the *tertiary*, or service-producing, sector of the economy.

In the next several chapters we will examine the active and inactive dimensions of the female reserve army in terms of the need for female labour. In the remaining chapters we will go on to consider the activation of the institutionalized reserve in terms of the growing need for married women to find employment to maintain the Canadian family's standard of living.

Chapter 5

The Female Reserve: Active and Inactive Dimensions

Writing in 1892, Jean Scott described how uncommon it was for Ontario married women living with their husbands to work outside their homes. Her research showed that most factories and stores had no married women and that the exceptions were widows and women whose husbands could not support them. She did find, however, that married women often worked in the summer months in canning factories.[1]

It is primarily the married women who do not work outside the home who constitute what I have designated as the institutionalized inactive reserve army of labour. These housewives have been and are available for use when the economy needs them.

It is a well-known fact that during World War II large numbers of women entered the labour force to replace the men who had joined the military service. The need for women workers under the conditions of war is described quite clearly by a pamphlet published in 1942 by the Dominion Bureau of Statistics entitled, accurately enough, *Reserve of Labour Among Canadian Women*.

There is abundant evidence that Canada's sources of labour

supply among men are rapidly approaching depletion. Employment is at the highest level in the country's history, approximately 5,000,000 persons of a population of 11,500,000 being in the armed services or in civilian occupations. . . . Since future accretions to the nation's labour force must come mainly from the ranks of women, a stock taking of Canada's womanpower is, at the present time, extremely important.[2]

With regard to married women it goes on to say that "for the alleviation of the manpower shortage interest centres chiefly upon the women not gainfully occupied," which is to say housewives. More specifically, it states:

. . . the largest source of future labour supply is among married women. . . . If the war is of long duration, with the absorption of more and more men into the armed forces on the one hand, and, on the other, an increasing tempo of war production, this source will have to be heavily drawn upon.[3]

The main interest centred on married women between fifteen and forty-four years of age in urban areas since it was this group that could be most easily mobilized.

Married women in this age group in urban localities provide a labour pool practically untapped. . . . It is in these large urban centres that day nurseries, community kitchens, laundries, etc., can be most easily provided.[4]

During the war period women were employed in many jobs that had formerly been done by men only. At the end of the war, however, men reclaimed these jobs and the form of reserve labour consisting of married women was deactivated. Those women who remained in the labour force moved or in many cases were forced to move into other occupations — "female" occupations.

For the most part, when male labour is plentiful, women are segregated into "female" jobs and do not compete directly for men's jobs. Since historically the kinds and numbers of jobs defined as "female" have been few, the majority of women have remained in the inactive reserve (with the exception of wartime). However, as female occupations grow in both number and kind, female labour is in greater demand. As a result of this demand a separate female labour market emerges and a greater part of the female inactive reserve becomes active.

Chart 5.1 represents the capitalist production process in its relation to female employment and illustrates the way the female reserve labour force operates.[5] At the top of the chart the mass of female workers who are employed in the various industries is shown. This mass is fed by (A) new workers finding jobs for the first time, by (G) those in the active reserve labour force who are unemployed, and by (H) housewives in the inactive reserve. Leaving employment are (F) retiring workers who have finished careers or women who leave employment for work in the home, (E) those who are laid off or displaced from industry through technological changes but continue to actively look for work, and (D) those who are displaced and do not continue to look for employment. The other streams that complete the picture are (B) new workers, married or unmarried, who look for jobs but are unable to find them and join the active reserve immediately, (J) those who give up after a period of seeking employment and move into the inactive reserve, and (C) married women who do not look for jobs outside the home but keep house and move into the inactive reserve immediately. Women workers (I) also move into the active reserve from the inactive reserve. Those are the workers who look for employment and are unable to find it right away or who do seasonal or part-time work.

This conception of the labour of women emphasizes women's permanent and integral connection to the capitalist production process by virtue of their status as employed or active-inactive reserve labour, it indicates that a supply of female labour is always available to be drawn on when the conditions of the capitalist economy dictate, and it differs from the traditional economic view that considers married women (as well as other people who are not defined officially as being in the labour force) as outside the process of production.[6] Married women, according to the traditional view, choose to enter the labour force only when it is in their own interest and that of their family to do so. The major factors influencing their choice (and therefore the supply of female labour) are their number of children, age, education, and husband's income and occupation.

CHART 5.1
Active and Inactive Female Reserve Army

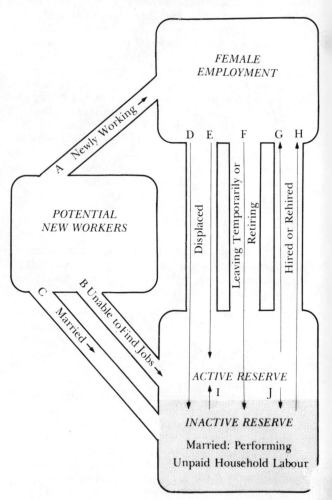

LEGEND FOR CHART 5.1

A   Newly Working
B   Unable to Find Jobs
C   Working Inside the Home Only
D   Displaced to Inactive Reserve
E   Displaced to Active Reserve
F   Leaving Temporarily or Retiring
G   Hired or Rehired from Active Reserve
H   Hired or Rehired from Inactive Reserve
I   Looking for Seasonal or Part-time Work
J   No Longer Looking for Employment

In the view presented here, the movement of women between the active and inactive reserves and into employment depends on the development of capital which, on the one hand, creates a demand for female labour to fill "female" occupations and, on the other hand, generates a supply of female labour by creating a need for married women to work for a wage.

In the previous chapter we saw clearly that some occupations employ predominantly women. We have evidence that the sex labels attached to "female" occupations are relatively stable and persist over time.[7] Thus if, as we have seen, workers are concentrated in certain occupations, then the demand for workers in these occupations could be seen as a crude indicator of the demand for female workers.[8]

It follows that an investigation of the changes occurring in the industrial and occupational structures should give us some insight into the demand for female labour in Canada. For example, as Oppenheimer suggests, if jobs that are defined as "female" are expanding rapidly, then that would be a rough indicator of the expansion in demand for female labour.[9] The first step is to look at the long-term trends in industrial and occupational growth in Canada.

Chapter 6

Demand for Female Labour: Changes in the Industrial Structure, 1901-1971

The distinction between *industry* and *occupation* is essentially that between what is produced and the kind of work done in production. An *industry* is defined as a group of establishments engaged in producing the same or similar kinds of products, whether the products are goods or services. The *industrial structure* refers to the distribution of the labour force according to the type of product the worker is involved in producing. An *occupation* is defined in terms of the kinds of tasks performed by the worker. The *occupational structure* refers to the distribution of the labour force by the kinds of work done.[1]

In the last seventy years major shifts have occurred in the industrial and occupational structures in Canada. These shifts took place as changing technology and the increased productivity of labour maximized profit in some industries, forcing capitalists to seek new areas to further expand their capital. Eventually this need to expand brought capitalists into new areas of production and fostered the development of new products as well. To fully understand the shifts in industrial and occupational structures and how they affect female labour it is important to see them in terms of a changing product as well as changing technology and increased productivity.

As the main aim of the capitalist is to accumulate more and more capital, to do so he must extend to the fullest the market where commodities are exchanged. The first step in creating a gigantic market is to transform the production of all goods into the commodity form.[2]

In the early stages of industrial capitalism in Canada there was a limited number of commodities in circulation. Most families lived on farms. Although some basic items were bought, manufacturing was still in its infancy, and the family was still the central productive unit.

Farm families usually built their own homes as well as constructing many of their home furnishings. Food production and the production of clothing for the most part were carried on within the home. In fact, the farm family was quite self-sufficient. It wasn't long, however, before the newly emerging capitalism made its presence felt in the areas of food processing, home construction, and the production of clothing, household articles of all sorts, tools, and other implements. The range of commodity production began to extend rapidly.

At the same time that manufacturing and processing industries were on the increase in the cities, the farm was becoming capitalized; that is, mechanized farm production was overtaking the older labour-intensive methods, and farm labour was producing more. This meant that less labour power was needed on the farm and some was "freed" to move to cities where it was needed in manufacturing industries.

In Canada as early as the period from 1901 to 1911 a decline in the number of farm units was underway in the long-settled areas of the Atlantic regions, although agriculture was still expanding in the unsettled areas of the Prairies and British Columbia.[3]

Over the years the decline [in agriculture] ...accelerated as competition and the rapid expansion of capital investment in

agriculture . . . forced the weak or undercapitalized farm out
of business.[4]

As farm capitalization increased, farm employment and
farm incomes decreased in relative terms.

> Thus while there has been only a slight increase in acreage
> cultivated between 1931 and 1961, farm capitalization has
> increased by almost 450 per cent. At the same time the farm
> labour force has declined by almost 50 per cent. . . . While
> productivity increased by 60 per cent between 1948 and
> 1958, income increased by only 5 per cent.[5]

By 1901 two-fifths (40.2%) of the labour force was employed in agriculture, and farm employment was declining
steadily so that by 1941 it gave work to only one-quarter
(24.0%) of the labour force and by 1961 it had dropped to
one-tenth (10.2%). The 1971 census shows that by that year
employment in agriculture had further declined to one-
twentieth (5.6%) of the work force.[6]

In his discussion of the creation of a relative surplus population Marx described this phenomenon.

> As soon as capitalist production takes possession of agricul-
> ture, and in proportion to the extent to which it does so, the
> demand for an agricultural labouring population falls
> absolutely. . . . Part of the agricultural population is therefore
> constantly on the point of passing over into an urban or
> manufacturing proletariat, and on the look-out for circum-
> stances favourable to this transformation.[7]

According to Marx, those who have been displaced,
"whether this takes the more striking form of the repulsion
of labourers already employed, or the less evident but not
less real form of the more difficult absorption of the additional labouring population through the usual channels,"
become surplus population available for employment in
other sectors of the economy.[8]

Frank Denton describes this process in Canada.

> The decline of agriculture as a source of employment re-
> leased large quantities of manpower for work in other sectors
> of the economy. . . . This was especially evident in the case of
> the children of farm families who left in large numbers to
> seek employment in the cities, towns, and villages once they
> had finished school.[9]

Many of the first workers to leave agriculture were

women. According to Genevieve Leslie:

> many farmers' daughters saw little future for themselves in
> older sections of the country where all the land had been
> settled. There were fewer single, independent farmers left to
> marry; as a result, rural women moved in great numbers to
> the cities.[10]

Once in the city these women were usually drawn into the
industries related to those tasks they had previously performed in the home. These were domestic and personal
service industries, where they worked mainly as servants,
and manufacturing industries, where they were in garment,
textile, and food-processing industries.[11]

As more people moved from country to city in order to
find work, their former self-sufficient lifestyle was eroded.
Men worked in factories, and in many cases the availability of
cheap manufactured goods made it more economical for
working-class women to sell their labour power to buy goods
rather than to make goods at home.

Other social forces were also at work to undermine home
crafts. For example, fashion and style dictated to the
younger generation through advertising (and the educational process emphasized) "store-bought" as opposed to
"homemade" goods. High status belonged to those who
could buy things, no longer to those who could make them.[12]
As a result of these and other factors, more goods were
transformed into commodities and a major shift occurred
away from resource-extracting and toward goods-
producing industries. As this occurred more women entered
the labour force.

The shift from agriculture to manufacturing was com-
pleted between 1941 and 1951 when agriculture began to
show a decrease in the number as well as the percentage of
people employed. The manufacturing sector then became
the largest area of employment in Canada, edging out agriculture 26.2% to 15.9% (see table 6.1 in Appendix B).

As the manufacturing industries were growing, that is, as
more goods were transformed into commodities and as
labour became more productive, the capitalist system gener-
ated new needs. The more commodities that were produced,
the more had to be consumed, thus creating a need for new

markets and marketing techniques including advertising, transportation, and selling of products. The need for financing and recording these transactions also increased. In other words, as productivity increased, the need to distribute and service those commodities produced by the manufacturing sector increased. These changes had an important effect on female labour. According to a Labour Department research monograph:

> Economic, social, and technological changes in the past half century have played a part in the growth in number of women workers. The increasing mechanization of production processes, with consequent dilution of skills, has resulted in the replacement, in some industries, of craftsman by operatives, many of whom have been women. But the largest area of new demand for women workers has been in the clerical and service occupations, resulting from the growth of large business organizations and improved general prosperity.[13]

It was this increasing emphasis on producing services, then, that gave rise to the demand for female labour.

The major source of employment for women in the early years in Canada was in the domestic service industry (which was outside of capitalist production). The shift from primary to secondary industries opened up some opportunities in manufacturing industries, primarily clothing, textiles, and food production. The greatest boost to female employment, however, came with the capitalist expansion of tertiary or service-producing industries, which now employ the majority of working women (see table 6.2 in Appendix B). Service industries duplicated many of the jobs women did as family members and as domestic servants, so that with the growth of the service sector, much of the production for which women were responsible became part of the capitalist production process.

Capitalism created a need not only for services related to the increased output of the manufacturing industries, but also for services supplied to people directly. Where in preindustrial Canada women provided most of the social services used by the family, with the move from rural to urban areas their services as teachers and nurses were no longer adequate for the needs of emerging capitalism. As Judi Coburn puts it, "in this new [urban] setting, the family could not provide the disciplined, literate, healthy worker that industry required, so the state stepped in."[14]

As the family declined with regard to these social functions, the void was filled by institutions created for this purpose. For a price these institutions provide the services once supplied (in many cases) by women in the home. The care and responsibility of people for one another has become increasingly institutionalized. Every aspect of life has become marketable. There are schools for the young, homes for the elderly, and hospitals for the sick, disabled, and mentally ill. As these services are removed from the home to institutions, new sources of labour power must be found to provide them. Often the labour power, like the tasks, comes from the home in the form of female labour.

By 1961 it was the service industries, not the manufacturing industries, that employed the largest percentage of the total labour force (25.4%). And by 1971 the percentage had risen even further to 31.1% (while agriculture employed only 5.6% and manufacturing industries, 19.8%). Clearly, then, technological change, the increased productivity of labour, and a shift in products produced under capitalism in Canada have led to major shifts among industries and sectors of the economy.

Significant changes have taken place within industries also. For example, the rise of large corporations and the expansion of the role of the state under monopoly capitalism have led to large, highly bureaucratized structures. These in turn have resulted in new jobs arising, others expanding, and some declining or disappearing altogether. Both the shifts among industries and within them have tended to favour the rise of white-collar occupations and a concomitant demand for female labour.

As we turn our attention now to the occupational structure, our aim is to discover more specifically to what extent shifts in industry and corresponding shifts in occupational composition have affected the demand for female labour.

Chapter 7

Demand for Female Labour: Changes in the Occupational Structure, 1901-1971

The two greatest changes in the Canadian occupational structure since 1901, quite closely related to the shifts among and within industries discussed in the last chapter, are the shifts away from agricultural occupations and toward white-collar jobs. The significance of these changes can best be understood by considering what the structure would have looked like if the occupational composition of the work force had not changed but rather had grown on the basis of the 1901 occupational configuration. By 1969 there would have been over three and one-quarter million farmers and farm workers instead of only one-half million. There would have been only one and one-quarter million white-collar workers instead of the three and one-half million actually employed.[1]

The proportion of the labour force as well as the number of workers employed in primary occupations in general has declined steadily since 1901 (from 44.4% to 7.7% in 1971). Manual occupations have levelled off in the percentage of workers employed, although the numbers employed in these occupations continue to increase. Within manual occupations there has been a general shift from unskilled to skilled labour. Service occupations (which are not to be confused with service industries) are still growing numerically and have increased only slightly in percentage terms.[2] The greatest increase is in white-collar occupations which now employ the largest number of people as well as the largest percentage of the labour force. These occupations have grown enormously from 15.2% in 1901 to 42.5% in 1971. Within the white-collar segment, the group which has shown the largest rate of expansion over this period is that of clerical workers (see table 7.1 in Appendix B). None of these changes should be surprising considering the growth of service industries, on the one hand, and the increasing reliance of all industry groups on technology and the bureaucratic method of organization, on the other hand.

If we consider the trends in the occupational *growth* for the male and female labour force (see tables 7.2a and 7.2b in Appendix B), we find that the only similarity is that both the men's and women's white-collar jobs increased in proportion to other occupations from 1901 to 1971 (men's jobs, from 14.1% to 33.1%; women's jobs, from 23.6% to 59.8%). On the other hand, the percentage of women in manual occupations dropped (from 30.6% to 10.1%) while that of men in those occupations grew and then levelled off in that period (from 32.5% to 39.2%). The percentage of women in service occupations declined (from 42.0% to 15.2%), while that of men increased (from 2.9% to 9.2%) in that time period. In primary occupations the percentage of females increased slightly and then returned to the 1901 figure (3.8%), while the percentage of males has sharply declined since 1901 (from 50.5% to 9.9%).

The occupational *distribution* is also considerably different for men and women. In 1901, there were 50.5% of male workers employed in primary occupations and 32.5% in manual jobs. Primary occupations remained the largest group and manual occupations the second largest until 1931, although the primary occupations were declining and the manual occupations increasing. By 1941 both were employing approximately the same percentage of the male labour force, 37.0%. During that time white-collar jobs for men were on the increase. By 1951 manual occupations, employing 42.9% of the male labour force, had solidly taken over first place from primary jobs, and the white-collar group had become second with 25.8% of the employed males. Although the percentage of manual jobs for men decreased slightly, to 39.2%, and male white-collar employment increased slightly, to 33.1%, their respective positions remained the same to 1971 (see table 7.2b).

The largest percentage of the female work force (42.0%) was in service occupations in 1901 and the second largest (30.6%) was in manual occupations. By 1911 service occupations still employed the largest percentage (37.6%), but the percentage employed in white-collar occupations had become second (29.9%). The percentage of women employed in service occupations had dropped to second place (27.0%) by 1921 and more had become employed in white-collar jobs (47.9%). This remained the case to 1971 as white-collar jobs increased to 59.8% and service occupations declined to 15.2%.

For the most part, then, since 1901 the majority of women in the Canadian labour force have been in service and white-collar occupations. Service occupations have always been among the largest employers of women in Canada. Most women who were in service occupations at the turn of the century were in domestic service, one of the few occupations open to them at the time, although many women preferred factory jobs to domestic service if they had a choice. Immigrant women, who had the fewest choices, were an important source of domestic labour and were usually over-represented in domestic jobs. For example, in 1911 immigrant women made up 24.1% of the female labour force but formed 35.0% of the female work force in domestic and personal service.[3] By 1971 immigrant women, compared to Canadian-born women, were still proportionately over-represented in service, production, and a variety of other processing and materials-handling occupations.[4]

As industrialization increased, those employed in domestic service declined. This was so partly because new female occupations were coming into existence and partly because many of the tasks done by domestic servants were being taken over by enterprises that contracted to do household maintenance. The rise of these new companies meant new job opportunities for women, although in many cases women were doing the same kind of work they had done in domestic service. For example, the domestic servant who, among other things, did laundry in her employer's home could work in a commercial laundry. This kind of job was preferred by women because their work and their work time was clearly established as it was not in domestic service.

Employing a woman in such a company was also advantageous for the capitalist because he could make a profit from her day's labour as he could not when she sold her labour power directly to the domestic employer. Until this time domestic service workers had not been a part of capitalist production. Leslie describes the effect of industrialization under capitalism on domestic service workers.

> Domestic service, like domestic labour in general, declined in status with the progress of industrialization. It was not considered an integral part of the economy, and to a large extent was excluded from economic and political discussion. It was "non-productive" service labour; it took place in the home and depended upon a personal relationship between employer and employee; it involved no significant outlay of capital and produced no direct profit. In a society based on the production of commodities for sale and profit, domestic labour was progressively devalued as production was removed from the home.[5]

Today many women are still in domestic and related services such as baby-sitting and house cleaning. Some are hired directly by the employer but more and more are being hired through profit-making agencies.

Although service occupations still employ the second largest number of women, the proportion of women to men in these occupations has dropped considerably since 1901 (see table 7.3 in Appendix B). This is due partly to the increase in protective service occupations, which are almost entirely male, and partly to the fact that many women who would once have gone into domestic service jobs are now moving into the rapidly rising and relatively new "female" occupations within the white-collar category.

As we have already seen, white-collar jobs are the most rapidly growing occupations in the labour force. It is also true that women are performing a rising share of this white-collar work. In large part this has been caused by the growing predominance of women in the most rapidly expanding segment of the white-collar area — clerical work. In the early nineteenth century, clerical workers were generally men, who had a higher status and made considerably more money than factory workers. Most of the duties they performed would today be classified as "managerial." Clerical workers as we now know them are a new stratum having little continuity with the privileged clerical workers of the past.

Graham Lowe points out that the growing division of labour and routinization of work within offices were major factors that brought about the substitution of females for males in Canadian offices. The "feminization" of clerical occupations was already apparent at the turn of the century. Today, the majority of clerks are women, who receive low wages, little self-fulfilment, and limited opportunities for promotion.[6] In 1901 women filled 22.1% of all clerical occupations, but by 1971 this figure had soared to 68.4% (see table 7.3).

Clerical work as we now know it is largely a product of the period of monopoly capitalism, according to Braverman. As small enterprises grew into large corporations, office work — accounting and recordkeeping, planning and scheduling, correspondence and interviewing, filing and copying— expanded until each function was separated into different sections or departments of the corporation. Functions such as keeping records of workers and material, tasks once performed by the owner and a small number of clerk-managers, are now done by many people in separate planning, purchasing, and engineering sections.[7]

In producing corporations where commodities in the form of goods and services are made and sold, these offices are ... subsidiary and complementary to the productive processes carried on elsewhere in the same corporation. But with the development of monopoly capitalism came the extraordinary enlargement of those types of enterprises which, entirely separated from the process of production, carry on their activities either chiefly or entirely through clerical labor.[8]

Banks and credit agencies are clear examples of these types of enterprises. Below the level of managers, employees consist mainly of clerks and cleaning staff. Most of these employees are women. Other examples of enterprises where the clerical character of the labour process is enormous are advertising and travel agencies, employment agencies, and government offices of public administration.[9]

The female share of sales occupations as well as that of clerical occupations has risen considerably over the seventy-year period. Clerical and sales occupations are the two relatively new "female" occupational groups (see table 4.5). Women make up the majority of those employed in the largest occupations in each of these groups, namely stenography and sales clerking. Other occupations which have been traditionally "female" such as nurses' aide jobs, nursing, and teaching have also grown enormously in terms of the number of women employed.

From this examination of the data we see that as capitalism has developed in Canada it has brought about changes in the industrial and occupational structures which have favoured the growth of those occupations defined as "female." As "female" occupations have expanded, the demand for women workers has increased. This increase in turn has contributed to the activation of the institutionalized inactive reserve in Canada.

Chapter 8

The Supply of Female Labour

What forces are pushing Canadian women into the active reserve and into the labour force? The bulk of the institutionalized inactive reserve, as we have discussed, is made up of married women who are living with their husbands. By considering factors that activate the female reserve we are essentially focussing on pressures that push *housewives* into the labour force.

The average family in Canada has been maintained by the husband's wage. His wage was expected to buy the necessary commodities converted by the housewife into the family's subsistence. If the husband's wage is insufficient to buy the commodities necessary to meet a reasonable standard of living in Canada, then the housewife has two alternatives to prevent the family's standard of living from declining. First, she can intensify her labour in the home; that is, she can cook more and use fewer of the costly prepared foods, mend rather than buying new things, shop more carefully, and generally try to stretch her husband's wage. Second, she can seek employment outside the home if jobs are available.

THE ENTRANCE OF MARRIED WOMEN INTO THE LABOUR FORCE

An increasing number of married women are taking the

alternative of working outside their homes rather than intensifying their labour in the home because under present conditions in Canada they can accomplish more in economic terms by doing so. The data show that married women in Canada have been entering the labour force in increasingly larger proportions (see table 1.1 in Appendix B). In 1931 the labour force participation rate of married women was only 3.5%. The 1941 census showed only a slight increase to 4.5%. The percentage more than doubled in 1951 to 11.2% and doubled again in 1961 to 22.0%. By 1971 the percentage of all married women participating in the labour force had risen to 37.0%.

This increase of married women has altered the composition of the female labour force. By 1961 married women made up a larger proportion of the female labour force (49.8%) than single women (those never married, 42.3%), although they composed a lesser proportion than single, divorced, and widowed women combined (single and other categories, 50.2%). However, by 1971 the percentage of married women in the labour force (59.1%) had increased to the point where it was greater than the combined percentage of single, divorced, and widowed women in the labour force.[1]

When the housewife takes a job outside the home it means an increase in the cost of maintaining the family. For example, there is the cost of day care or a baby-sitter if there are young children in the family. More clothes, transportation, and laundry are needed for working, while an increased reliance on prepared foods and labour-saving devices occurs as married women must meet their household obligations in a shorter period of time. There is a trade-off of the increased cost of the family's maintenance resulting from the housewife working outside the home for the additional income her employment brings in.[2] However, it would not make economic sense for her to work if only an equal exchange between lost domestic labour and the housewife's wage took place. What occurs is that the extra cost of maintaining the family, which results from the housewife's working outside the home, is lower than the wage received. Thus it is economically advantageous for a housewife to enter the labour force.[3]

That housewives have a small portion of their wage left after costs are deducted is certainly not because women's wages have risen. On the contrary, women's wages in Canada have declined over the years relative to men's wages. Neil MacLeod, conducting a trend analysis for the period 1946 through 1968, compared men's and women's earnings in manufacturing industries. He concluded that on the whole no improvement had been made over the twenty-two-year period that he had examined.

> The situation is as stagnant as a polluted river. The consistency of the pay differentials is particularly interesting in view of the large increases in the number of women working and the technological advances which have opened up new kinds of jobs and produced major changes in the nature of work performed in most, if not virtually all industries.[4]

Between 1967 and 1972 the dollar difference between full-time workers increased in every occupation. For example, in 1967 the difference between women's and men's salaries in clerical occupations was $1,925, and in 1972 it was $2,807. The average earnings of male employees in clerical occupations increased by $2,221 from 1967 to 1972 compared with $1,339 for women.[5] Lynn McDonald says, "Women who work full-time in Canada earn on the average about 60 per cent as much as male full-time workers." Moreover, "The gap in wages and salaries between women and men is *increasing* — in all the provinces, and any way you look at it."[6]

When the earnings of female and male full-time, full-year workers are compared for 1971, we do indeed find that women earn only 59% of what men earn (see table 8.1 in Appendix B). This is the same ratio that existed in 1961, showing that the gap has not narrowed. When the wages of all female and male wage earners in 1971 (including those who work part-time) are compared, the gap increases. In 1961 women earned 54% of what men earned, but by 1971 this had declined to 50%.

The gap between women's and men's wages is sometimes explained as resulting from the occupational segregation of women. Morley Gunderson examined what the overall ratio of women's to men's earnings would look like if women had the same occupational distribution as that of men while retaining their own earnings within an occupation. He found that if women workers were distributed among occupations in the same way as men were, but continued to receive the wage rates paid to women, then the gap between men's and women's wages would increase.

> Adjusting for differences in occupational distribution by sex does not by itself raise the ratio of female to male earnings. For the broader occupational groupings [those of table 8.1], occupational desegregation would not reduce the wage gap unless accompanied by more equal wages within each occupation. Equalizing the occupational distribution would, to a large extent, transfer women from clerical and teaching occupations, where the earnings differential is small to primary and blue collar jobs, where the earnings gap is large.[7]

Gunderson also estimated what women would earn if they were paid according to the pay structure for males. He found that "paying both sexes according to the male pay structure would raise female earnings from 60 percent of male earnings to 93 percent. The remaining 7 percent gap is due to differences in age, marital status, education, and residence between males and females."[8]

If the overall price of women's labour has declined relative to the overall price of men's labour, then it cannot be a higher wage that explains why it makes economic sense for a housewife to work outside the home. Why is it, then, that a woman has a small amount of her wage left after she deducts the extra cost of maintaining the family which results from her going out to work? The explanation is found in the fact that productivity in the industrial sector has risen significantly relative to the productivity in the domestic sphere. As capitalism develops, the housewife has to work more hours in the home to make up for one hour spent in producing wage goods. Since this is the case, a woman working outside the home can earn enough to replace her lost domestic labour and still have a small portion of her wage to use for her family's needs.[9]

PRODUCTIVITY OF INDUSTRIAL LABOUR AND DOMESTIC LABOUR

Although the productivity of domestic labour has increased in absolute terms, it has fallen behind the productivity of industrial labour. According to the *Report* of the Royal Commission on the Status of Women:

> Comparison with much earlier studies suggests that hours spent on housework have not decreased as much as one would expect in a technological age. The question therefore arises whether or not housework has been influenced by the same forces of technological change that have transformed and continue to alter the rest of the economy.[10]

The answer to that question is that housework has *not* been influenced by the same forces of technological change that have altered the rest of the economy. This is because domestic labour has no direct relation to capital. Domestic labour is not paid a wage and does not create surplus value: therefore, the capitalist has no interest in increasing its productivity.

Within industrial production, on the other hand, any increase in the productivity of labour increases surplus value, raises profits, and gives one capitalist a competitive advantage over another. The result has been that new technology and new ways of organizaing and dividing labour have been introduced into industrial production to increase productivity while the domestic labour process has advanced only to the extent that new technology is introduced into the household via commodity consumption.

The industrialization process involves definite changes in social organization as well as technology.[11] Although technology has been introduced into Canadian households, new ways of organizing and dividing household labour to increase its efficiency have not been introduced. Household labour has been mechanized but not industrialized, and as a result its productivity has risen in absolute terms but has fallen behind relative to the productivity of industrial labour.

Today women can accomplish their household work in less time than they could before because they have machinery and because many of the services once performed by domestic labour are being displaced or altered by the state and by the production and service sector of the capitalist economy. The *Report* of the Royal Commission on the Status of Women describes this phenomenon:

> Mechanization of the old processes of spinning, weaving, cutting and sewing has transferred the manufacture of clothing from the home to the factory. Commercial laundries have taken over much of the cleaning. Truck-gardening, canning, freezing and precooking have lessened the importance of the home in the production, preservation, and preparation of food. . . . Other functions, which had stayed in the home, have been greatly altered. Meal preparation has been changed by the introduction of a wide variety of appliances. New quick-freezing techniques for fresh food, along with improvements in canning and pre-cooking techniques and the addition of chemical fortification to foods, make it possible for the family to eat varied and nutritious meals with much less preparation in the home.[12]

The advance of technology and the rising productivity of labour in the industrial sector has lowered the cost of many consumer goods. The lower cost has put them almost within reach of the majority of people. At one time only the wealthy could afford these products and they were considered by most people to be luxuries. However, as more goods are produced in a shorter time, mass consumption of these goods becomes imperative for the ongoing capitalist system. New needs are created among the population so that the greater number of goods produced have a ready market. These needs are created partly through advertising but mainly through failing to develop alternatives or through encouraging the erosion of existing alternative ways of doing things. For example, the automobile is a necessity and not a luxury if an adequate public transportation system does not exist. In the household, refrigerators and stoves are no longer luxuries. Most households in Canada today find it *necessary* to have a stove and refrigerator (see table 8.2 in Appendix B).[13]

According to the census of 1941, at that time half of Canadian households had no installed baths or showers and 45% of households had no inside toilets. Few people would question the necessity of these facilities today. Jenny Podoluk gives other examples of items that were considered necessities by the 1960s. She mentions such items as television sets and automobiles. By the late 1960s even welfare officials recognized that expenditures on television ownership should not disqualify recipients from receiving assistance.[14]

As capitalism develops, what was once a luxury for a few becomes a necessity for the majority. Women are not working for labour-saving devices which are luxuries or "extras." They are working for necessities (which must be constantly replaced as a result of planned obsolescence) that cannot be purchased by one wage and in most cases are just beyond the purchasing power of the second wage (note, for example, the rise in the use of credit).[15]

THE ECONOMIC NECESSITY FOR MARRIED WOMEN TO WORK OUTSIDE THE HOME

Evidence that married women *need* to work outside the home can be found by examining several Canadian studies dealing with women in the labour force. In 1955-56, for example, the Canadian Department of Labour conducted a survey in eight Canadian cities of married women working outside their homes.[16] One of the aims of this survey was to discover why these married women were working. The reasons became apparent when the researchers considered the husband's income alone and then his income combined with that of his wife. When the husband's income alone was considered, only 14% of the families had as much as $4,000 to live on. However, when the wife's income was also considered, half of the families (51%) had incomes of $4,000 or more.[17]

In 1954, as many as 43% of all non-farm families, whether there was one income or more, were in the "$4,000 and over" group.[18] With the husband's income alone, the families in this survey would have been well below a cross section of Canadian urban families in income; but with the addition of the wife's income, these families compared favourably with others. The authors concluded, "The extreme importance of the economic motive in keeping these married women at work outside the home is one of the most outstanding findings of this survey."[19]

In 1961, data on husband-and-wife family income distribution again confirmed the importance of the wives' earnings. Half of all husband-and-wife families (including those in which wives worked outside the home and those in which wives did not) had incomes of $5,000 or more. In families where the wives did not work outside the home, 45% had incomes of $5,000 or more. In families where the wives did work outside the home, almost two-thirds (64.8%) had incomes (including the wives' earnings) of over $5,000. However, when the earnings of the wives are excluded, only slightly more than one-third (36.1%) of those families with working wives had incomes of over $5,000. Removing the wives' earnings from consideration results in an income distribution which is lower than that of families with non-working wives. It would appear, then, that husbands in families with non-working wives have higher incomes than husbands in families with working wives.[20] Clearly married women whose husbands have low incomes are compelled to find employment outside the home.

Again in 1971 data suggest that the lower the family's income (excluding the wife's earnings) the greater the likelihood that a married woman will work outside the home. Almost half (47%) of the women whose family incomes were less than $3,000 (excluding her own earnings) participated in the labour force. When family incomes (excluding wives' earnings) were higher, the economic need for married women to work outside the home decreased and so did their participation in the labour force (see table 8.3 in Appendix B).

These data, then, illustrate the effect of an underlying structure; that is, women participate in the labour force as a result of the class conditions. At the same time the data indicate that not all women of a given economic class are entering the labour force. This fact can be explained by reference to factors which mitigate the effects of the structure and discourage or prevent women from participating despite the economic pressures of capital accumulation and its effects on class conditions. Such factors are, for example, the lower availability of "female" occupations in the rural areas of the country, lack of adequate child care facilities, negative attitudes of husbands or communities toward women working outside the home, and the ability of women to intensify labour and stretch their husbands' wages through growing their own food where possible, mending clothes, etc. But the presence of these factors does not deny the class conditions that structure women's participation in the labour force in general — as a group. The focus of this analysis is on these structural conditions rather than on individual motivational concerns. A structural-class outlook, of course, does not deny the importance of motivational factors in explaining variations from the central trend of women's labour force participation, but it does necessitate the exclusion of these factors for the sake of making explicit the usefulness of this type of analysis.

In summary, then, between 1951 and 1971 the participation rate of married women in the labour force more than tripled. It is the married women whose husbands earned the least that were most likely to be working outside the home. The question is: Do these women work to get the "extras" that their husband's income won't buy, or are they working because their husband's wage can no longer buy what is *necessary* to maintain the family at a reasonable standard of living? The evidence points strongly to the latter explanation: married women work in order to maintain the family's economic position.

Women at Work in Canada: 1964 indicated that many women were working out of need:

> Since the thirties the level of living of the population, including the "real" incomes that sustain it, has risen remarkably. The standard of living — that level at which people feel they are comfortably off and not deprived of anything important — has increased also; the availability of a wide range of consumer goods has assisted in the latter process. Yet a considerable proportion of male wage-earners, in fact the major-

ity, do not earn the $6,000 or so per year that is necessary to move consumption much beyond food, clothing, and shelter. For many Canadian families, however, the earnings of the wife added to those of the husband just succeed in bringing total income up to a fairly comfortable level.[21]

According to Leo Johnson, since 1951 there has been a growing disparity between higher and lower wage earners despite the rise in per capita income.[22] This disparity has contributed toward the restructuring of family earning patterns. Multi-earner families have increased enormously since 1951 until by 1971 almost two-thirds (64.9%) of all Canadian families had more than one income recipient.

Hugh Armstrong and Patricia Armstrong have convincingly argued that married women's "earnings supplement the family's income, thus helping the family maintain its financial status in spite of the increasing disparity for individuals in general."[23] They illustrated the growing inequality in individual income distribution between 1951 and 1971. Over this twenty-year period it was found that all individuals with income, all wage earners, and all unattached individuals with income in the lowest earning three-fifths of the population received a decreasing share of the total income. At the same time the top two-fifths received an increasing share. The top two-fifths of wage earners increased their share of the total income from 65.3% in 1951 to 69.8% in 1971. A corresponding decline was experienced by the other three-fifths of the population so that by 1971, two-fifths of all wage earners earned 70% of the total income while the remaining three-fifths earned only 30% (see table 8.4 in Appendix B).[24]

In comparing the distribution of income among Canadian families, however, the pattern that exists for individuals does not repeat itself. Rather, the families in the lowest two-fifths experienced only a slight decline in proportion of the total income and the families in the middle one-fifth increased their share. The top one-fifth, on the other hand, had a reduction in their proportion of the total income.[25]

It is married women's earnings which prevent the family income distribution from matching that of the individual income groups. As our earlier discussion illustrated, women whose husbands have low incomes are most likely to work.

Therefore, the fact that these women are working explains why the bottom two-fifths did not decline significantly in income and why the middle one-fifth improved their positions slightly. Women in the highest income groups were least likely to work outside the home, and therefore the decline in the share of the total income experienced by the highest one-fifth can be explained by this fact.

It would appear, then, that as the standard of living in Canada rises, married women whose husbands earn low incomes must work outside the home to maintain their relative standard of living. That is, married women don't work in order to close the gap between rich and poor families. Rather, they work to prevent the difference from increasing. To stay at home and try to stretch their husband's wage is no longer a viable alternative. To maintain what is now considered a reasonable standard of living, families must purchase a growing number of goods and services which are rapidly becoming indispensable. For their families to be in a financial position to purchase them, many wives must work outside the home. The existence of these goods and services is a prerequisite for women taking outside employment. At the same time it is the production of these goods and services that women themselves once produced in the home which has led to the expansion of "female" occupations. In other words, married women are "free" to work because of the creation of necessities which in fact determine their need to work.[26] These, then, are the conditions that activate the institutionalized inactive form of the female reserve army.

Chapter 9

Summary
and Conclusion

On the basis of Marx's theory of capitalist development, the conditions under which women work have been explained and analysed with reference to Marx's concept of a reserve army. I have argued that women in Canada are a reserve army of labour. By revising and expanding the concept I have suggested that women in Canada do meet the preconditions of cheapness and availability as well as the principal condition of competition — the defining characteristics of a reserve army of labour.

'I have shown that women are available because with the advent of industrial capitalism they were defined out of the labour market. While male labourers became commodity producers, women, as a group, became domestic workers. Women's labour is cheap because part of the value of their labour has been included in the price of their husband's or future husband's labour. Women without husbands have not been able to, and still cannot, support a family adequately. In economic terms the majority of women under capitalism have little alternative but to marry.

With respect to competition this analysis shows that women do not compete for men's jobs since women are segregated into certain occupations. The data do not show the existence of one labour market where men and women compete. Rather there are two distinct labour markets — a female and a male labour market. While women do not directly compete for men's jobs within *a* labour market they do compete with other women within a *female* labour market. Thus, with respect to the female labour market, women do compete for women's jobs and in doing so meet the principal condition of reserve labour. Furthermore, although women do not compete directly for men's jobs, the existence of a distinct female labour market has an indirect competitive effect on male labour. As women meet these conditions of cheapness, availability and competition, there appear to be sound analytic grounds for considering women as a reserve army of labour in Canada.

In examining the historically specific forms of the female reserve in Canada it became apparent that some women have always been part of the active reserve forms as Marx described them. However, women, and married women in particular, constitute an additional form, one that I have identified as an institutionalized inactive reserve army. This concept denotes that women's domestic labour is held in an inactive reserve form which over the years has become institutionalized. The most obvious historical example of the use of this inactive reserve was during the world wars.

Conditions in Canada are once again activating this form of the reserve labour, but on a permanent basis. On the one hand, a changing industrial and occupational structure has led to the expansion of female occupations, creating a demand for female workers. This demand, of course, in the short term, will be affected by downturns in the economy during which women will be among the last hired and first fired. On the other hand, with the capitalist penetration of the household, commodities once considered luxuries have become necessities and traditional ways of doing things have become obsolete. In order to buy the goods and services now necessary to maintain an average Canadian standard of living women are compelled to enter the wage labour force. At the same time it is the existence of these goods and services which frees women (within limits) to work outside the home.

It is under these conditions that the inactive reserve is activated in Canada. And it is the activation of the institutionalized reserve army which accounts for the increase in female labour force participation.

According to my structural analysis, then, the growth in female labour force participation is seen as a relatively stable phenomenon, one which has implications for the Canadian labour force as a whole as well as women's place in it. The increasing participation of married women is necessary in order to maintain existing standards of life within the family. This means that the capitalist has succeeded in spreading direct exploitation throughout the family. Now, in order to earn the cost of reproducing and maintaining the family, both husband and wife must sell their labour power in the capitalist labour market.

In conclusion I would point out that in rejecting the consumer choice model I have essentially rejected an approach that centres on subjective conditions and individual choices to explain behaviour. The consumer choice approach reduces the difficulties working women face to individual problems and by implication directs women to seek primarily individual solutions.[1]

This research has demonstrated that women's participation in wage labour is not a matter of immediate situational factors but rather of prestructured alternatives which direct the decisions that women are compelled to make. This approach allows women to see the structural basis of their position. As women become conscious of these objective conditions it is highly probable that they will move beyond individual solutions — to collective action for changing the structures which limit them. The increasing militancy of women may, indeed, be on the historical agenda.

Appendix A

Problems in Using Census Data

Census data are not without limitations. A major limitation of decennial census data is that there are only a few observations, and some changes between decades are missed. For example, the decline in female labour force participation following World War II took place between census years and did not show up in the census figures. These latter figures show a continual increase of women entering the labour force.

Table A.1 shows that in the census year 1941 women were 22.3% of the labour force. By the 1951 census, 22.5% of the labour force was female. In between these years, however, the female proportion had risen to a high of 31.4% in 1945 and had dropped to 22.7% in 1946.

Other problems stem from the fact that continual improvements have been occurring in Canada's data-collecting efforts. While these improvements are both necessary and important, they have created difficulties in the use of the data. The major problems as stated by Warren E. Kalbach and Wayne W. McVey, Jr. are: "(1) the periodic disruption of historical series, (2) discontinuities created by revision of data collection area boundaries, (3) changes in basic concepts, and (4) updating of specific indicators of social and economic conditions."[1] It is the increasing awareness of

specific problems within the census data that creates the
need for more refined measures and often brings about
modifications of previously used concepts.

TABLE A.1

**Women as a Percentage of the Labour
Force by Selected Years, 1891-1971**

Year	Percentage
1891	17.8
1901	16.0
1911	18.1
1921	22.4
1931	19.1
1938	20.4
1939	20.6
1940	21.3
1941	22.3
1942	24.2
1943	30.3
1944	31.0
1945	31.4
1946	22.7
1951	22.5
1961	26.7
1971	32.4

SOURCE: Lorna R. Marsden, "Why Now? The Mirage of
Equality," p. 13.

A problem which is more specific to my use of the data
arises from the fact that new information needs and the
modifications in existing concepts are defined and established to meet the needs of those for whom the census data
are primarily collected, namely, government agencies and
business. For my research different kinds of data are required in addition to what is available. For example, in an
investigation of the use of labour as a reserve army, it is
important to know how many workers hold more than one

job. Up to the present the census has not provided information on multiple job-holding. Persons with more than one job are classified as holding the job in which the most time is spent.

Despite the problems, however, census data are still the best available Canadian sources for illustrating the concepts used in this study. With regard to my use of secondary data sources, the reader is cautioned that many of the questions posed in this research have had to be answered indirectly, using what data do exist.

A central focus of the study is on the occupational structure and woman's place in it. In terms of the data problems discussed, it is important to point out that while some attempts are made to account for the effects of changes in occupational definitions in the census, there is no attempt to account for the effects of changes in procedures other than calling the fact to the reader's attention.

Where possible I have made use of studies in which adjustments in the data have already been made. One such work is Noah M. Meltz's *Manpower in Canada, 1931-1961*. In this study Meltz has analysed the changing occupational structure for a thirty-year period. His discussion of the difficulties he encountered as a result of the changing classification system clearly highlights some of the problems in using census data.[2]

All of the difficulties that Meltz points to when discussing changes between the 1931 through 1961 censuses are more than doubled when it comes to the 1971 census. The greatest problem stems from the fact that whereas the 1951 census had sixteen occupational groups and the 1961 census had thirteen, the 1971 census had twenty-one such groups. The difficulty in linking the 1971 statistics to earlier censuses is reflected in the fact that Statistics Canada has not yet produced the historical tables comparing the 1971 figures to previous census figures.

Since the historically comparative aspect of the 1971 census has been delayed, I have found it necessary to combine occupational groups myself in order to make them even roughly comparable to those used by Meltz.[3] Table A.2 describes the way the 1971 data are compared with the 1951 classification used by Meltz.

TABLE A.2

Occupational Categories, 1901-1961 and 1971

1901-1961	*1971*
White-Collar	
Proprietary and Managerial	Managerial, Administrative and Related Occupations
Professional	Occupations in Natural Sciences, Engineering and Mathematics
	Occupations in Social Sciences and Related Fields
	Occupations in Religion
	Teaching and Related Occupations
	Occupations in Medicine and Health
	Artistic, Literary, Recreation and Related Occupations
Clerical	Clerical and Related Occupations
Commercial and Financial	Sales Occupations
Manual	
Manufacturing and Mechanical	Processing Occupations
	Machine and Related Occupations
	Product Fabricating, Assembling and Repairing Occupations
Construction	Construction Trades Occupations
Labourers	No Equivalent Category
Transportation and Communication	Transport Equipment Operating Occupations
	Materials Handling and Related Occupations

	Other Crafts and Equipment Operating Occupations
Service	Service Occupations
Primary	
Agriculture	Farming, Horticultural and Animal Husbandry Occupations
Fishing, Trapping	Fishing, Hunting, Trapping and Related Occupations
Logging	Forestry and Logging Occupations
Mining, Quarrying	Mining and Quarrying including Oil and Gas Field Occupations

There were some obvious problems in combining certain 1971 occupational groups for comparison as shown in table A.2. However, since there exists no overall guide that would allow me to make *all* of the correct adjustments, I decided to combine occupations at only the most general level which, although allowing for only a very crude comparison, would not mislead the reader into thinking that a satisfactory adjustment had been made.

Besides the census data, other major sources of statistics used in this research were the Department of Labour's annual publication, *Women in the Labour Force*, and *Women at Work in Canada*. Data are also drawn from other government surveys such as surveys of consumer finances, *A Study of Married Women Working for Pay in Eight Canadian Cities*, *Occupational Histories of Married Women Working for Pay*, and the *Report* of the Royal Commission on the Status of Women in Canada.[4]

Appendix B

Tables

TABLE 1.1

Female Labour Force Participation, Census Years 1931-1971[1]

	Participation Rate				Married Women as a Percentage of Total Women[2] in Labour Force
Year	Married	Single	Other	Total	
1931	3.5%	43.8%	21.3%	19.3%	10.0%
1941	4.5	47.2	17.3	20.3	12.7
1951	11.2	58.3	19.3	24.1	30.0
1961	22.0	54.1	22.9	29.5	49.8
1971	37.0	53.5	26.5	39.9	59.1

1. Statistics from the 1931 census are for the age group 10 and over. Statistics from the 1931-51 censuses are for the age group 14 and over. Statistics from the 1961 and 1971 census are for the age group 15 and over. Figures exclude those on active military service; Newfoundland is included from 1951 on; the Yukon and Northwest Territories are not included.

2. Including permanently separated.

SOURCES: *1961 Census, Advance Report* N. AL-1, Catalogue No. AL-1, Catalogue No. 94-500: Byron Spencer and Dennis Featherstone, *Married Female Labour Force Participation*; and Statistics Canada, *1971 Census*, Vol. III, Catalogue 94-706, table 14; Catalogue 94-774, table 8.

TABLE 4.1
Women in Disproportionately Female Occupations 1901-1971

Year[2]	Females as a Percentage of Total Labour Force	Disproportionately Female Occupations[1]		Ratio of Observed to Expected
		Percentage of Female Labour Force Expected in These Occupations[3]	Percentage of Female Labour Force Observed in These Occupations	
1901	13	17	85	5.0
1911	13	23	91	4.0
1921	15	26	92	3.5
1931	17	24	88	3.7
1941	20	28	90	3.2
1951	22	28	84	3.0
1961	27	37	88	2.4
1971	34	36	76	2.1

1. A "disproportionately female" occupation is one in which women form a higher proportion of the workers in the occupation than they do of the labour force as a whole.
2. These census data have not been adjusted and therefore are not entirely comparable. Since I have always used the most detailed occupational classification much of the change could be the result of a more or less refined set of occupational categories.
3. This is the percentage of the female labour force that would have been observed in these occupations if their sex composition had been the same as the sex composition of the labour force as a whole.

SOURCE: *Censuses of Canada, 1921, 1931, 1941, 1951, 1961, 1971.*

TABLE 4.2
Percentage of Female Labour Force in Occupations Having Various Concentrations of Women, 1901-1971

Percentage Occupation Female	1901[2]		1911		1921		1931	
	Ob-served	Ex-pected[1]	Ob-served	Ex-pected	Ob-served	Ex-pected	Ob-served	Ex-pected
90+	15	2	14	3	13	2	46	8
80+	54	8	24	5	24	4	52	9
70+	67	10	54	10	45	8	62	12
60+	69	11	61	11	47	8	64	12
50+	75	12	67	13	68	14	68	13

Table 4.2 continued

Percentage Occupation Female	1941		1951		1961		1971	
	Ob-served	Ex-pected	Ob-served	Ex-pected	Ob-served	Ex-pected	Ob-served	Ex-pected
90+	43	9	22	5	25	7	26	9
80+	44	9	36	9	32	9	36	14
70+	54	12	45	11	49	15	43	17
60+	65	15	57	15	56	18	61	26
50+	70	17	67	20	77	29	65	28

1. This is the percentage of the female labour force that would have been observed in these occupations if the sex compositions of these occupations had been the same as the sex compositions of the labour force as a whole.

2. These census data have not been adjusted and therefore are not entirely comparable. Since I have always used the most detailed occupational classification, much of the change could be the result of a more or less refined set of occupational categories.

SOURCE: *Censuses of Canada, 1921, 1931, 1941, 1951, 1961, 1971.*

TABLE 4.3

**Occupations in Which 70% or More
of the Workers Were Women, 1901**

Occupation	Percentage of Female Work Force in Occupation	Females as a Percentage of Total Work Force in Occupation
Dressmakers and seamstresses	13.5	100.0
Servants	34.2	83.7
Housekeepers	3.2	87.0
Teachers	13.0	78.0
Milliners	1.8	99.4
Paperbox and bag makers	0.1	70.8
Nurses	0.1	100.0
Office employees not elsewhere classified	3.7	79.6

SOURCE: *Census of Canada, 1921*, table 1.

TABLE 4.4

Occupations in Which 70% or More of the Workers Were Women, 1971

Occupation	Percentage of Female Labour Force in Occupation	Females as a Percentage of Total in Occupation
OFFICE OCCUPATIONS	18.6	92.4
Supervisors: stenographic and typing occupations	0.1	82.9
Secretaries and stenographers	8.1	97.4
Typists and clerk-typists	2.9	95.6
Tellers and cashiers	3.5	91.2
Insurance, bank, and other finance clerks	0.5	78.4
Office machine operators	0.6	79.2
Electronic data processing equipment operators	0.7	74.0
Library and file clerks	0.9	82.2
Receptionists and information clerks	1.4	92.6
NURSING AND THERAPY OCCUPATIONS	6.9	87.7
Supervisors: nursing occupations	0.5	92.8
Graduate nurses, except supervisors	3.1	95.8
Nurses in training	0.3	95.9
Nursing assistants	0.8	91.9
Nursing aides and orderlies	1.8	74.4
Nursing, therapy, and related assisting occupations not elsewhere classified	0.3	82.1
Physiotherapists, occupational and other therapists	0.2	81.7

Table 4.4 continued

TEACHING OCCUPATIONS	*4.5*	*81.3*
Elementary school teachers	4.1	82.3
Elementary and secondary school teaching and related occupations not elsewhere classified	0.4	74.6
Teachers of exceptional students	0.1	73.5
PERSONAL SERVICE OCCUPATIONS	*3.0*	*93.5*
Chambermaids and housemen	0.4	95.5
Baby-sitters	0.7	96.6
Personal service occupations not elsewhere classified	1.9	92.0
MISCELLANEOUS OCCUPATIONS		
Librarians and archivists	0.2	76.3
Nuns and brothers	0.1	91.4
Dietitians and nutritionists	0.1	95.0
Radiological technologists and technicians	0.2	73.4
Medical laboratory technicians	0.5	75.6
Dental hygienists, assistants, and technicians	0.3	76.6
Telephone operators	1.0	96.0
Other sales occupations not elsewhere classified	0.1	76.7
Waiters, hostesses, and stewards, food and beverage	3.6	82.9

Table 4.4 continued

Food and beverage pre- paration and related services not else- where classified	0.4	84.7
Supervisors: occupations in lodging and other accomodations	0.4	70.6
Apparel and furnishings service occupations	0.1	73.9
Winding and reeling occupations - textiles	0.1	73.2
Electronic equipment fabricating and assem- bling occupations	0.2	72.3
Tailors and dressmakers	0.6	73.0
Sewing machine operators, textile and similar materials	1.9	90.1
Inspecting, testing, grading occupations: fabricating, assembling and repairing, textile, fur and leather products	0.1	84.3
Fabricating, assembling and repairing occupations: textile, fur and leather products, not elsewhere classified	0.3	72.3

Note: Two occupations that were 70% female were omitted because they did not consist of 0.1% of the female labour force. They were "dancers and choreographers" and "occupations in library, museum, and archival sciences."

SOURCE: *Census of Canada, 1971*, Catalogue 94-788, table 1.

TABLE 4.5

Selected Occupations, 1901-1971

	Number of Females in Occupation	Percentage of Female Labour Force in Occupation	Females as a Percentage of Total in Occupation
(a) Dressmakers and Seamstresses			
1901	32,065	13.5	100.0
1911	29,567	8.1	99.8
1921	17,933	3.7	100.0
1931	10,411	1.6	100.0
1941	10,885	1.3	100.0
1951	14,237	1.2	98.3
1961	15,516	0.9	95.8
1971	16,555	0.6	73.0
(b) Servants/Maids and Related Workers			
1901	81,493	34.3	83.7
1911	98,128	26.9	78.1
1921	88,825	18.1	77.7
1931	143,043	20.2	94.0
1941	148,999	17.9	95.2
1951	88,775	7.6	89.1
1961	120,392	6.8	88.0
1971	89,290	3.0	93.5
(c) Nurses, Graduate and in Training			
1901	280	0.1	100.0
1911	5,475	1.5	97.8
1921	21,162	4.3	99.0
1931	31,898	4.8	100.0
1941	38,283	4.6	99.4
1951	49,780	4.2	98.1
1961	81,868	4.7	96.7
1971	113,780	3.8	96.0
(d) Teachers, Elementary and Secondary			
1901	30,863	13.0	78.0
1911	34,063	9.3	80.6
1921	49,795	10.2	81.9

Table 4.5 continued

	Number of Females in Occupation	Percentage of Female Labour Force in Occupation	Females as a Percentage of Total in Occupation
1931	64,709	9.7	78.0
1941	64,465	7.7	74.6
1951	74,319	6.4	71.7
1961	118,594	6.7	70.7
1971	180,515	6.1	66.4

(e) Office Employees, Clerical Workers

1901	8,749	3.7	22.8
1911	30,625	8.4	39.4
1921	78,824	16.1	43.4
1931	116,927	17.6	45.1
1941	152,216	18.6	50.1
1951	321,809	27.7	56.7
1961	508,021	28.9	61.7
1971	940,180	31.8	68.5

(f) Saleswomen/Salesclerks

1901	2,729	1.2	15.4
1911	24,321	6.7	21.4
1921	36,189	7.4	26.4
1931	56,413	6.8	30.9
1941	68,456	6.8	41.1
1951	95,670	8.2	52.9
1961	133,773	7.6	53.6
1971	169,250	5.4	66.0

Notes: a. The 1931 figure includes dressmaker's apprentices. In 1941, 1951 and 1961, it is specified that the dressmakers are those not in a factory. In 1971 the category "tailors" was included with dressmakers.

b. This category is called "servants" from 1901 to 1921, "domestic services, n.e.s." in 1931 and 1941, and "hotel, cafe and private household workers" in 1951. In 1961 I combined "maids and related

Table 4.5 continued

workers, n.e.s." and "baby-sitters." In 1971 I combined the occupations "chambermaid and houseman," "baby-sitters" and "personal service occupations, n.e.s." While these occupations are not equivalent, their similarities allow us to trace the decline in this kind of personal service work.

c. The occupations "nurses" and "nurses in training" became separate categories in 1931.

d. The occupations "elementary school teacher" and "secondary school teacher" were distinguished in 1971.

e. Clerical work was categorized by industry rather than by type of work from 1901 to 1921. Thus it was necessary to use the occupational group rather than specific occupations in order to convey the growing importance of clerical occupations. However, from 1931 on I have included the more important occupations in the group. Some occupations had to be combined for a greater degree of comparability. For 1961, "stenographers" and "typists and clerk-typists" were combined. In 1961 there was no occupation "office clerks." Because of the number of women in the new category "clerical occupations, n.e.s.," it was assumed that women who were categorized in 1951 as "office clerks" must be in this new category in 1961. For 1971 "secretaries and stenographers" and "typists and clerk-typists" were combined and "bookkeepers and accounting clerks" and "tellers and cashiers" were combined. Also "general office clerks" and "other clerical and related occupations, n.e.c." were combined in order to remain consistent with the 1961 categorization.

f. This occupation was called "salesmen and saleswomen" from 1901 to 1931, "salespersons in stores" in 1941, and "salesclerks" from 1951 to 1971.

SOURCE: *Censuses of Canada 1921, 1931, 1941, 1951, 1961, 1971.*

TABLE 6.1

Percentage of the Total Labour Force in Major Industrial Groups, 1931-1971

Industry	1931	1941	1951	1961	1971
PRIMARY	*33.0*	*31.5*	*21.3*	*14.2*	*8.3*
Agriculture	28.7	25.8	15.9	10.1	5.6
Forestry and Fishing	2.5	3.5	3.5	2.3	1.1
Mining	1.8	2.2	2.0	1.9	1.6
SECONDARY	*27.9*	*28.8*	*32.9*	*31.0*	*26.0*
Manufacturing	20.4	23.4	26.2	23.6	19.8
Construction	7.5	5.4	6.7	7.6	6.2
TERTIARY	*39.1*	*39.5*	*44.7*	*52.7*	*57.7*
Electricity, Gas and Water	0.7	0.6	1.2	1.1 ⎫	⎫
Transportation and Communication	8.1	7.0	8.3	7.9 ⎭	7.8 ⎭
Trade	10.1	11.2	13.6	14.7	14.7
Finance	2.4	2.2	2.8	3.6	4.2
Service	17.8	18.6	18.8	25.4	31.1
Community and Business Service	6.4	6.6	8.3	12.1	⎫
Government Service	2.6	2.8	3.9	5.7	23.7
Recreation Service	0.5	0.4	0.6	0.6	⎬
Personal Service	8.3	8.8	6.0	7.0	⎭
Public Administration and Defence	—	—	—	—	7.4

Table 6.1 continued

	1931	1941	1951	1961	1971
INDUSTRY NOT STATED	0.0	0.2	1.1	2.1	7.9
Total per cent	100.0	100.0	100.0	100.0	100.0
Total number (in thousands)	3917.6	4196.0	5214.9	6342.3	8626.9

SOURCE: Noah M. Meltz, *Changes in the Occupational Composition of the Canadian Labour Force, 1931-1961*, table A-5; *Census of Canada, 1971*, Catalogue 94-787, table 1.

TABLE 6.2

Percentage of the Female and Male Labour Force in Major Industrial Groups, 1931-1971

Industry	Females					Males				
	1931	1941	1951	1961	1971	1931	1941	1951	1961	1971
PRIMARY	*3.8*	*2.5*	*3.4*	*4.9*	*4.2*	*39.0*	*38.7*	*26.5*	*17.8*	*10.5*
Agriculture	3.6	2.3	3.0	4.5	3.8	33.8	31.6	19.6	12.2	6.5
Forestry and Fishing	0.1	0.1	0.2	0.1	0.1	3.0	4.3	4.4	3.1	1.7
Mining	0.1	0.1	0.2	0.3	0.3	2.2	2.8	2.5	2.5	2.3
SECONDARY	*18.7*	*22.0*	*24.1*	*18.1*	*14.6*	*26.1*	*29.8*	*35.3*	*35.2*	*32.0*
Manufacturing	18.5	21.8	23.6	17.4	13.7	18.5	23.3	26.8	25.3	23.0
Construction	0.2	0.2	0.5	0.7	0.9	7.6	6.5	8.5	9.9	9.0

Table 6.2 continued

TERTIARY	*76.9*	*74.9*	*71.4*	*74.6*	*71.0*	*29.8*	*30.3*	*36.9*	*44.5*	*50.8*
Electricity, Gas, Water	0.3	0.2	0.5	0.5	{3.8	0.7	0.7	1.4	1.4	{9.8
Transportation and Communication	3.4	2.4	4.2	{3.6		7.8	7.3	8.7	8.6	
Trade	12.8	13.5	18.2	17.1	15.7	9.3	10.5	12.3	14.1	14.2
Finance	3.7	3.4	5.5	5.9	6.2	2.1	1.8	2.0	2.7	3.1
Service	56.7	55.4	43.0	47.5	45.2	9.9	10.0	12.5	17.7	15.3
Community Service	{22.2	{19.8	{20.2	{23.6	{39.7	{3.1	2.9	3.4	4.9	—
Business Service		* 0.4	1.6	2.4			0.3	1.0	1.7	—
Personal Service	2.3	3.3	4.6	5.3		2.9	3.3	4.4	6.8	—
Recreation Service	0.4	0.4	0.6	0.6		0.5	0.4	0.5	0.6	—
Government Service	31.8	31.5	16.0	15.6		3.4	3.1	3.2	3.7	—
Public Administration and Defence	—	—	—	—	5.5	—	—	—	—	8.4
INDUSTRY NOT STATED	*0.6*	*0.6*	*1.1*	*2.4*	*10.2*	*5.1*	*1.2*	*1.3*	*2.5*	*6.7*
Total per cent	**100.0**	**100.0**	**100.0**	**100.0**	**100.0**	**100.0**	**100.0**	**100.0**	**100.0**	**100.0**
Total number (in thousands)	**665.3**	**832.8**	**1163.9**	**1760.5**	**2961.2**	**3252.3**	**3363.1**	**4051.0**	**4581.8**	**5665.7**

SOURCE: Noah M. Meltz, *Manpower in Canada, 1931-1961*, tables A.2 and A.3; *Census of Canada, 1971*, Catalogue 94-787, table 1.

TABLE 7.1

Percentage of the Total Labour Force in Major Occupational Groups, 1901-1971

Occupation	1901	1911	1921	1931	1941	1951	1961	1971
WHITE-COLLAR	15.2	16.8	25.1	24.5	25.2	32.4	38.6	42.5
Proprietary and Managerial	4.3	4.6	7.2	5.6	5.4	7.5	7.9	4.3
Professional	4.6	3.7	5.5	6.1	6.7	7.4	10.0	12.7
Clerical	3.2	3.8	6.8	6.7	7.2	10.8	12.9	16.0
Commercial and Financial	3.1	4.7	5.6	6.1	5.9	6.7	7.8	9.5
MANUAL	32.2	36.1	31.3	33.8	33.4	37.7	34.9	29.2
Manufacturing and Mechanical	15.9	13.7	11.4	11.5	16.0	17.4	16.4	13.7
Construction	4.7	4.7	4.7	4.7	4.7	5.6	5.3	5.6
Labourers	7.2	12.0	9.7	11.3	6.3	6.8	5.4	3.2
Transportation and Communication	4.4	5.7	5.5	6.3	6.4	7.9	7.9	6.7
SERVICE	8.2	7.7	7.1	9.2	10.5	8.6	10.8	11.2
Personal	7.8	7.5	5.8	8.3	9.3	7.4	9.3	8.9
Protective and Other	0.4	0.2	1.3	0.9	1.2	1.2	1.5	2.3
PRIMARY	44.4	39.4	36.3	32.5	30.6	20.1	13.1	7.7
Agriculture	40.3	34.3	32.7	28.8	25.8	15.9	10.2	5.9
Fishing, Trapping	1.6	1.3	0.9	1.2	1.2	1.0	0.6	0.3
Logging	0.9	1.5	1.2	1.1	1.9	1.9	1.3	0.8
Mining, Quarrying	1.6	2.3	1.5	1.4	1.7	1.3	1.0	0.7

Table 7.1 continued

Occupation	1901	1911	1921	1931	1941	1951	1961	1971
NOT STATED	—	—	0.2	—	0.3	1.2	2.6	8.5
NOT ELSEWHERE CLASSIFIED	—	—	—	—	—	—	—	0.9
All Occupations								
per cent	100.0	100.0	100.0	100.0	100.0	100.0	100.0	100.0
number (in thousands)	1782.8	2723.6	3164.3	3917.6	4196.0	5214.9	6342.3	8626.9

SOURCES: Noah M. Meltz, *Changes in the Occupational Composition of the Canadian Labour Force, 1931-1961*, table A.1; *Census of Canada, 1971*, Catalogue 94-788, table 1.

TABLE 7.2a

Percentage of the Female Labour Force in Major Occupational Groups, 1901-1971

Occupation	1901	1911	1921	1931	1941	1951	1961	1971
WHITE-COLLAR	23.6	29.9	47.9	45.4	44.6	55.4	57.4	59.8
Proprietary and Managerial	1.2	1.6	2.0	1.6	2.0	3.0	2.9	2.0
Professional	14.7	12.5	19.0	17.7	15.6	14.4	15.6	17.8
Clerical	5.3	9.1	18.5	17.7	18.3	27.4	28.6	31.7
Commercial and Financial	2.4	6.7	8.4	8.4	8.7	10.6	10.3	8.4
MANUAL	30.6	28.0	21.1	16.9	18.5	19.4	13.3	10.1
Manufacturing and Mechanical	29.6	26.4	18.0	12.7	15.4	14.6	9.9	7.4
Construction	—	—	—	—	—	0.1	—	0.1
Labourers	0.5	0.1	0.1	1.8	1.4	1.8	1.2	0.9
Transportation and Communication	0.5	1.5	3.0	2.4	1.7	2.9	2.2	1.7
SERVICE	42.0	37.6	27.0	34.0	34.4	21.3	22.5	15.2
Personal	42.0	37.5	26.0	33.9	34.3	21.1	22.2	14.9
Protective and Other	—	0.1	1.0	0.1	0.1	0.2	0.3	0.3
PRIMARY	3.8	4.5	3.7	3.7	2.3	2.8	4.3	3.7
Agriculture	3.8	4.4	3.7	3.6	2.3	2.8	4.3	3.6
Fishing, Trapping	—	0.1	—	0.1	—	—	—	—
Logging	—	—	—	—	—	—	—	—
Mining, Quarrying	—	—	—	—	—	—	—	—

Table 7.2a continued

	1901	1911	1921	1931	1941	1951	1961	1971
NOT STATED	—	—	0.3	—	0.2	1.1	2.5	10.8
NOT ELSEWHERE CLASSIFIED	—	—	—	—	—	—	—	0.4
All Occupations per cent	100.0	100.0	100.0	100.0	100.0	100.0	100.0	100.0
All Occupations number (in thousands)	237.9	364.8	489.1	665.3	832.8	1163.9	1760.5	2961.2

SOURCES: Noah M. Meltz, *Changes in the Occupational Composition of the Canadian Labour Force, 1931-1961*, tables A.2, A.3; *Census of Canada, 1971*, Catalogue 94-788, table 1.

TABLE 7.2b

Percentage of the Male Labour Force in Major Occupational Groups, 1901-1971

Occupation	1901	1911	1921	1931	1941	1951	1961	1971
WHITE-COLLAR	*14.1*	*14.8*	*21.0*	*20.2*	*20.4*	*25.8*	*31.4*	*33.1*
Proprietary and Managerial	4.8	5.0	8.2	6.4	6.2	8.8	9.8	5.5
Professional	3.1	2.4	2.9	3.7	4.5	5.4	7.9	10.0
Clerical	2.9	3.0	4.7	4.4	4.5	6.0	6.9	7.6
Commercial and Financial	3.3	4.4	5.2	5.7	5.2	5.6	6.8	10.0

Table 7.2b continued

Occupation	1901	1911	1921	1931	1941	1951	1961	1971
MANUAL	*32.5*	*37.3*	*33.1*	*37.2*	*37.1*	*42.9*	*43.2*	*39.2*
Manufacturing and Mechanical	13.8	11.7	10.2	11.3	16.2	18.2	18.8	17.1
Construction	5.4	5.5	5.5	5.6	5.8	7.2	7.3	8.5
Labourers	8.2	13.8	11.4	13.2	7.6	8.1	7.1	4.4
Transportation and Communication	5.1	6.3	6.0	7.1	7.5	9.4	10.0	9.2
SERVICE	*2.9*	*3.1*	*3.4*	*4.1*	*4.6*	*4.9*	*6.3*	*9.2*
Personal	2.6	2.8	2.1	3.0	3.2	3.4	4.3	5.8
Protective and Other	0.3	0.3	1.3	1.1	1.4	1.5	2.0	3.4
PRIMARY	*50.5*	*44.8*	*42.3*	*38.5*	*37.6*	*25.1*	*16.4*	*9.9*
Agriculture	45.9	38.9	38.1	33.9	31.7	19.7	12.5	7.2
Fishing, Trapping	1.8	1.5	1.1	1.5	1.5	1.3	0.8	0.5
Logging	1.0	1.8	1.4	1.3	2.3	2.5	1.7	1.2
Mining, Quarrying	1.8	2.6	1.7	1.8	2.1	1.6	1.4	1.0
NOT STATED	—	—	0.2	—	0.3	1.3	2.7	7.4
NOT ELSEWHERE CLASSIFIED	—	—	—	—	—	—	—	*1.2*
All Occupations per cent	**100.0**	**100.0**	**100.0**	**100.0**	**100.0**	**100.0**	**100.0**	**100.0**
All Occupations number (in thousands)	**1544.9**	**2358.8**	**2675.3**	**3252.3**	**3363.1**	**4051.0**	**4581.8**	**5665.7**

SOURCES: Noah M. Meltz, *Changes in the Occupational Composition of the Canadian Labour Force, 1931-1961*, tables A.2, A.3; *Census of Canada, 1971*, Catalogue 94-788, table 1.

TABLE 7.3

Females as a Percentage of the Total Labour Force in Each Major Occupational Group, 1901-1971

Occupation	1901	1911	1921	1931	1941	1951	1961	1971
WHITE-COLLAR	20.6	23.8	29.5	31.5	35.1	38.1	41.3	48.5
Proprietary and Managerial	3.6	4.5	4.3	4.8	7.2	8.9	10.3	15.7
Professional	42.5	44.6	54.1	49.5	46.1	43.5	43.2	48.1
Clerical	22.1	32.6	41.8	45.1	50.1	56.7	61.5	68.4
Commercial and Financial	10.4	19.2	23.1	23.1	29.4	35.2	36.7	30.4
MANUAL	12.6	10.4	10.4	8.5	11.0	11.5	10.6	12.0
Manufacturing and Mechanical	24.8	25.9	24.3	18.7	19.1	18.8	16.8	18.5
Construction	*	*	0.1	*	0.2	0.3	0.2	0.9
Labourers	0.9	0.1	0.2	2.6	4.4	6.0	6.1	10.1
Transportation and Communication	1.4	3.5	8.4	6.5	5.3	8.2	7.9	8.7

Table 7.3 continued

SERVICE	68.7	65.3	58.9	63.0	65.1	55.4	57.8	46.2
Personal	71.7	67.2	68.9	69.6	72.9	64.2	66.4	57.4
Protective and Other	2.7	6.8	11.9	2.1	1.8	3.1	5.1	3.9
PRIMARY	1.1	1.5	1.6	1.9	1.5	3.1	9.2	16.4
Agriculture	1.2	1.7	1.7	2.1	1.8	3.9	11.7	20.9
Fishing, Trapping	0.2	0.8	0.2	1.0	0.5	0.5	1.1	1.9
Logging	—	—	—	—	—	*	0.2	2.1
Mining, Quarrying	*	*	*	—	*	*	*	0.6
NOT STATED	—	—	23.0	18.0	15.1	20.5	25.8	43.3
NOT ELSEWHERE CLASSIFIED	—	—	—	—	—	—	—	13.6
All Occupations	**13.3**	**13.4**	**15.5**	**17.0**	**19.8**	**22.3**	**27.8**	**34.3**

* less than 0.05%   — none

SOURCE: Noah M. Meltz, *Changes in the Occupational Composition of the Canadian Labour Force, 1931-1961*, table A-4; *Census of Canada, 1971*, Catalogue 94-788, table 1.

TABLE 8.1

**Ratio of Women's Earnings to Men's Earnings,[1]
All and Full-time Wage Earners,
by Occupation, 1961 and 1971**

| Occupation | 1961 Census[2] | | 1971 Census | |
	All Wage Earners	Full Year[3] Full-time	All Wage Earners	Full Year[3] Full-time
Managerial Professional[4]	.46	.56	.49	.56
Clerical	.61	.74	.59	.67
Sales	.35	.45	.34	.49
Service	.47	.47	.37	.50
Primary	.43	.60	.38	.47
Blue-collar[5]	.53	.59	.47	.53
Other	—	—	.47	.55
All occupations	.54	.59	.50	.59

1. Earnings figures are for wage and salary earners and exclude self-employed in unincorporated business. 1961 and 1971 ratios are not strictly comparable. In 1961, wage and salary data were collected, with fine breakdowns to the income level of $12,000, with an open-end class of $15,000 or more. For calculating averages, all incomes of $15,000 or more were given the value of $15,000. This means that, for occupations that had any incomes of $15,000 or more, the averages are too low. The groups most likely to be affected are the managerial and professional. In 1971, actual earnings were collected, so that the same bias does not exist in 1971 data.
2. 1961 occupational groupings are based on the 1951 census categories and are not directly comparable with the 1971 figures, which are based on the CCDO groupings (see notes to table 4.8 in Gunderson).
3. Worked 49-52 weeks for 35 or more hours per week.
4. 1961 figures are an unweighted average of the ratios for managers and professional and technical, used because the two groups had approximately equal numbers in 1961.
5. 1961 ratios are a weighted average of the ratios for transportation and communication with craft, production, and related workers. The latter ratio was weighted by 3 to reflect the fact that there were approximately 3 times as many craft,

Table 8.1 continued

production, and related workers as transportation and com- munication workers. 1971 figures consist of CCDO occupa- tions 81-95, which include crafts, production, transportation, communication, and construction workers.

SOURCES: 1961 data are derived from Sylvia Ostry, *The Female Worker in Canada*, table 16. Data for 1971 are from special 1971 census tabulations from Statistics Canada. Table from Morley Gunderson, "Work Patterns," p. 121. Reproduced by permission of the Minister of Supply and Services Canada.

TABLE 8.2

Percentages of Canadian Households Surveyed That Had Certain Household Equipment, 1948-1968[1]

Item	1948	1953	1958	1963	1968
Hot and cold running water	—	62.57	73.50	84.86	90.97
Gas or electric stove[2]	48.49	62.73	76.66	87.24	94.03
Mechanical refrigerator	29.26[3]	66.33[3]	86.24[3]	94.20	97.44
Home freezer	—	2.22	8.17	17.66	29.16
Electric washing machine	59.21	76.38	84.28	86.81	83.57
Vacuum cleaner	32.02	48.01	60.94	72.45	—
Electric sewing machine	—	23.43	36.30	49.03	—
Gas or electric clothes dryer	—	—	—	21.60	36.79
Automatic dishwasher	—	—	—	2.08	5.08
Floor polisher	—	—	—	—	55.01

Table 8.2 continued

1. Does not include households in the Yukon, Northwest
   Territories or on Indian reserves.
2. Includes piped and bottled gas and oil or kerosene.
3. Includes both gas and electric refrigerators. The number
   of gas refrigerators, however, dwindled rapidly, so that
   their exclusion from the statistics after 1958 probably
   makes little difference.
— No statistics available.

SOURCES: Dominion Bureau of Statistics, *Household
Facilities and Equipment.* (Ottawa: Queen's
Printer, 1948, 1953, 1958, 1963, 1968),
Catalogue 64-202. Table from Canada, Royal
Commission on the Status of Women in Canada,
Report, p. 34.

TABLE 8.3

**Labour Force Participation Rates of
Married Women Living with
Their Husbands, by Family Income
Minus the Wife's Wages, 1971**

Family Income Minus the Wife's Wages	Participation Rate of Wives
Under $3000	47%
3000-5999	44
6000-8999	44
9000-11,999	38
12,000-14,999	33
15,000 or over	27

SOURCE: Special 1971 census tabulations from Statistics
Canada. Table from Morley Gunderson,
"Work Patterns," table 4.3, p. 101. Reproduced by permission of the Minister of Supply
and Services Canada.

TABLE 8.4

Percentage Distribution of Total Income by 20% Groupings of Population, 1951-1971

Year	Lowest 20%	Second 20%	Third 20%	Fourth 20%	Highest 20%
ALL INDIVIDUALS					
1951[1]	3.2	9.2	17.4	25.2	45.0
1961[1]	3.1	8.9	17.2	26.0	44.8
1971	2.0	7.2	15.5	26.0	49.2
1971[2]	2.3	9.2	15.8	25.8	45.8
WAGE EARNERS					
1951[1]	4.2	12.0	18.6	25.0	40.3
1961[1]	3.7	11.7	18.7	25.6	40.3
1971	2.3	10.1	17.8	25.8	44.0
UNATTACHED INDIVIDUALS					
1951[1]	2.7	8.9	16.1	25.8	46.6
1961[1]	3.1	7.8	14.8	26.6	47.7
1971	2.9	8.0	14.9	25.8	48.5
1971[2]	3.3	9.2	15.8	25.8	45.8
FAMILIES					
1951[1]	6.1	12.9	17.4	22.4	41.1
1961[1]	6.6	13.5	18.3	23.4	38.4
1971	5.6	12.6	18.0	23.7	40.0
1971[2]	6.4	13.5	18.5	23.8	37.8

1. Excludes farm income.
2. Represents income after income taxes, but no other taxes, have been removed.

SOURCES: Canada, Dominion Bureau of Statistics, *Income Distributions*, Catalogue 13-529, tables 9 and 12; Canada, Statistics Canada, *Income after Tax, Distributions by Size in Canada, 1971*, Catalogue 13-210, p. 16. Table from Hugh Armstrong and Patricia Armstrong, "The Segregated Participation of Women in the Canadian Labour Force, 1941-1971," p. 381.

NOTES

Chapter 1

1. Canada, Royal Commission on the Status of Women in Canada, *Report*, p. 53.
2. Sylvia Ostry, *The Female Worker in Canada*, p.1.
3. Ibid.
4. Margaret Benston, "The Political Economy of Women's Liberation," pp. 13-27.
5. This is not to say that people do not make choices. "No one in his right mind — Marxist, mechanical materialist, or idealist — has ever denied that men make choices, ...The problem is and always has been to discover what determines the nature of the alternatives that are available to men, what accounts for the nature of the goals which they set themselves in different periods of historical development, what makes them will what they will in various societies at various times" (Paul A. Baran and Eric J. Hobsbawm, "The Method of Historical Materialism," p. 56).
6. See David M. Gordon, *Theories of Poverty and Underemployment*.
7. Karl Marx, *A Contribution to the Critique of Political Economy*, p. 12.
8. Ibid., p. 11.
9. This discussion is based on the exposition in Henry Veltmeyer, "Marx's Two Methods of Social Analysis," and Henry Veltmeyer, "The Methodology of Dependency Analysis."
10. Alice Clark, *The Working Life of Women in the Seventeenth Century*; Ivy Pinchbeck, *Women Workers and the Industrial Revolution, 1750-1850*.
11. Alice Henry, *Women and the Labour Movement*; and Edith Abbott, *Women in Industry*.

12. Janice Acton, Penny Goldsmith, and Bonnie Shepard, eds., *Women at Work: Ontario, 1850-1930.*

Chapter 2

1. A useful reference for this chapter is Paul M. Sweezy, *The Theory of Capitalist Development.* See especially chapter 5, "Accumulation and the Reserve Army."
2. *Capitalist* is used here as Marx used it — to represent capital: "As capitalist, he is only capital personified" (Karl Marx, *Capital,* p. 233).
3. Ibid., p. 216.
4. Ibid., p. 217.
5. Ibid., pp. 509-510.
6. A major factor in the shortening of the working day, of course, was the struggle of the working class. "The establishment of a normal working-day is the result of centuries of struggle between capitalist and labourer." ibid., p. 270.
7. Ibid., p. 628.
8. Ibid., p. 630.
9. Ibid., p. 632.
10. Ibid.
11. Sweezy, *The Theory of Capitalist Development,* p. 87.
12. Marx, *Capital,* p. 639.
13. Sweezy, *The Theory of Capitalist Development,* pp. 88-89.
14. Marx, *Capital,* p. 620.
15. Ibid., p. 641.
16. Ibid., p. 643.
17. Ibid.
18. Ibid., p. 644.
19. For elaboration see Sweezy, *The Theory of Capitalist Development,* chapter 1, "Marx's Method," esp. p. 18.
20. Marx, *Capital,* p. 640.

Chapter 3

1. Leo Johnson, "The Political Economy of Ontario Women in the Nineteenth Century," p. 14.
2. Ibid., p. 15.
3. Ibid., p. 16.
4. This type of society corresponds to conditions that Marx described as a precapitalist petty commodity formation, except

for our purposes we have laid greater emphasis on the role of women than Marx did.

5. For an elaboration of the changes in productive forces in Canadian society since the nineteenth century see R.T. Naylor, "The Rise and Fall of the Third Commercial Empire of the St. Lawrence"; H.C. Pentland, "The Development of a Capitalistic Labour Market in Canada"; and Stanley Ryerson, *Unequal Union*.

6. Eli Zarestky, "Capitalism, the Family, and Personal Life."

7. Margaret Benston, "The Political Economy of Women's Liberation," p. 16.

8. *Value* refers to *exchange value* unless otherwise stated.

9. *Socially necessary labour time* is the amount of time required to produce an article under the normal conditions of production and with the average degree of skill and intensity prevalent at the time. The introduction of modern machinery made a great difference to the socially necessary labour time needed to produce certain items (see chapter 2).

10. Karl Marx, *Capital*, p. 171.

11. Ibid., p. 172.

12. Paul Sweezy, *The Theory of Capitalist Development*, p. 61.

13. Marx, *Capital*, p. 171.

14. Ceta Ramkhalawansingh, "Women During the Great War," pp. 267-269.

15. Sylva Gelber, "The Compensation of Women," p. 11.

16. Sylva Gelber, "The Economic and Academic Status of Women in Relation to Their Male Colleagues," p. 39.

17. Canada, Royal Commission on the Status of Women in Canada, *Report*, p. 72.

18. According to Janice Madden, the employer's monopsony-type power arises from some combination of:
    (1) power which rests with one employer because he is the only employer within the market;
    (2) power which is shared by several employers who divide a heterogenous labor market so there is a limited number of employers per subdivision of the market;
    (3) power which is shared by employers of both sexes and by male laborers as a standard of a male supremacist society which "exploits" female laborers (Janice Madden, *The Economics of Sex Discrimination*, p. 69).

19. Marx, *Capital*, p. 535.

20. Ibid., pp. 535-537.

21. Ibid., p. 539.

22. Lori Rotenberg, "The Wayward Worker: Toronto's Prostitute

at the Turn of the Century," pp. 48-49.
23. Ibid., p. 49.
24. Sylva Gelber, "Women's Responsibility in the Search for Equality of Rights," p. 26.

Chapter 4

1. This part of the discussion applies a model used to determine the existence of a female labour market in the United States. See Valerie Kincade Oppenheimer, *The Female Labor Force in the United States,* chapter 3. In constructing my tables for this chapter, I have replicated those of Oppenheimer, using Canadian data.
2. Ibid., p. 68.
3. The ratio of observed to expected in Canada ranged from 5.0 in 1901 to 2.1 in 1971, while in the U.S. it ranged from 3.5 in 1900 to 2.1 in 1960 (see ibid., p. 69).
4. The Canadian findings are similar to Oppenheimer's findings for the U.S.
5. Karl Marx, *Capital,* p. 394.
6. Charles Lipton, *The Trade Union Movement of Canada: 1827-1959,* p. 58.
7. Leo Johnson, "The Political Economy of Ontario Women in the Nineteenth Century," pp. 28-30.
8. Alice Klein and Wayne Roberts, "Besieged Innocence," p. 222.
9. Renée Geoffroy and Paule Sainte-Marie, *Attitudes of Union Workers to Women in Industry.*
10. Canada, Royal Commission on the Status of Women in Canada, *Report,* p. 73.
11. Dorothy Smith and Lorna Marsden, "Equal Pay for Work of Equal Value."
12. Canada, Royal Commission on the Status of Women, *Report,* p. 72.
13. Kathleen Archibald, *Sex and the Public Service.*
14. Ibid., p. 31, n. 22.
15. Patricia Connelly, "Women in Trade Unions."
16. Morley Gunderson, "Work Patterns," p. 113.
17. Canada, Royal Commission on the Status of Women, *Report,* p. 103.
18. The same thing would happen to these women as Marx described happening to orphans and pauper children during his

time. He says of the children, "These are candidates for the industrial reserve army, and are, in times of great prosperity, as 1860, e.g., speedily and in large numbers enrolled in the active army of labourers" (Marx, *Capital*, p. 643).
19. Ontario Ministry of Community and Social Services, *It Pays to Work*.
20. Canada, Department of Labour, Women's Bureau. *Women at Work in Canada*, p. 20.

Chapter 5

1. Jean Thompson Scott, *The Conditions of Female Labour in Ontario*, University of Toronto Studies in Political Science (Toronto: 1892), p. 25, in Canada, Department of Labour, *Women at Work in Canada*, p. 2.
2. Canada, Dominion Bureau of Statistics, *Reserve of Labour Among Canadian Women*, p. 1.
3. Ibid., pp. 1-2.
4. Ibid., p. 2.
5. For a similar diagram showing how the reserve army operates with regard to the overall industrial process, see Paul M. Sweezy, *The Theory of Capitalist Development*, p. 91.
6. It is important to note that official definitions of unemployment in the capitalist labour market include only a part of what I am calling the active reserve army. Official definitions obscure the reserve nature of those who have not sought work within a specified limited period of time.
7. See for example Valerie Kincade Oppenheimer, *The Female Labor Force in the United States*.
8. Ibid., p. 65.
9. Ibid., p. 141.

Chapter 6

1. See Noah M. Meltz, *Manpower in Canada, 1931-1961*, and Sylvia Ostry and Mahmood A. Zaidi, *Labour Economics in Canada*.
2. Harry Braverman's very important book *Labor and Monopoly Capital* has influenced my work throughout, and this part of the discussion draws particularly on Braverman's argument concerning the development of a universal market under capitalism. See chapter 13, "The Universal Market," esp. pp.

271-276.

3. Leo A. Johnson, "The Development of Class in Canada in the Twentieth Century," p. 148.
4. Ibid.
5. Ibid., p. 149.
6. See Frank Denton, *The Growth of Manpower in Canada,* p. 61, and Canada, Statistics Canada, *1971 Census,* Catalogue 94-787.
7. Karl Marx, *Capital,* p. 642.
8. Ibid., p. 630.
9. Denton, *The Growth of Manpower,* p. 32.
10. Genevieve Leslie, "Domestic Service in Canada, 1880-1920," p. 90.
11. Canada, Dominion Bureau of Statistics, *Sixth Census of Canada, 1921,* vol. IV, table 1.
12. Braverman, *Labor and Monopoly Capital,* p. 276.
13. Canada, Department of Labour, *Women at Work in Canada,* p. 14.
14. Judi Coburn, " 'I See and Am Silent,' " p. 132.

Chapter 7

1. Sylvia Ostry and Mahmood A. Zaidi, *Labour Economics in Canada,* p. 87. See Valerie Kincade Oppenheimer, *The Female Labor Force in the United States,* chapter 5, "The Interaction of Demographic and Economic Factors in the Growth of the Female Labor Force," for her discussion of industrial and occupational shifts in the U.S.
2. Service industries include a great many occupations such as clerical, managerial and professional occupations; at the same time service industries do *not* include all the service occupations, some of which are to be found in the other industries.
3. Genevieve Leslie, "Domestic Service in Canada, 1880-1920," p. 96.
4. Monica Boyd, "The Status of Immigrant Women in Canada," pp. 228-244.
5. Leslie, "Domestic Service in Canada," p. 73.
6. Graham Lowe, "Trends in the Development of Clerical Occupations in Canada, 1901-1931."
7. Harry Braverman, *Labor and Monopoly Capital,* p. 299.
8. Ibid., p. 300.
9. Ibid., pp. 300-301.

Chapter 8

1. Much of the material in this chapter appears in another version in Patricia Marchak, ed., *The Working Sexes: Symposium Papers on the Effects of Sex on Women at Work* (Vancouver: Institute of Industrial Relations, University of British Columbia, 1977).

2. As *Women at Work in Canada: 1964* points out, the "married" category in these official statistics includes both married women who are living with their husbands and those who are separated. Since our interest is in married women living with husbands, it is important to exclude those women who are separated from their husbands and who need to work by virtue of being the only breadwinner (Canada, Department of Labour, *Women at Work in Canada: 1964*, p. 20). "The census does provide a count of married women living with their husbands who were in the labour force" (ibid). In 1961, 42.3% of the female labour force was made up of women who had never married, 44.9% of married women living with their husbands, and 12.8% of widowed, divorced, and separated women. In 1971, 33.4% of the female labour force was composed of women who had never married, 54.7% of married women living with their husbands, and 11.9% of widowed, divorced, and separated women. By 1971, then, more than half of the Canadian women working were married and living with their husbands (ibid., p. 21, table 8; and Canada, Statistics Canada, *1971 Census,* vol. 3, Catalogue 94-706, table 14).

3. See Wally Seccombe, "Domestic Labour — Reply to Critics," pp. 91-92.

4. Neil MacLeod, "Female Earnings in Manufacturing," p. 48.

5. Canada, Department of Labour, Women's Bureau, *Women in the Labour Force*, p. 70, table 6.

6. Lynn McDonald, "Wages of Work," p. 4.

7. Morley Gunderson, "Work Patterns," p. 122.

8. Ibid., pp. 122, 126.

9. Seccombe, "Domestic Labour — Reply to Critics," pp. 92-94. The following section draws on Seccombe's argument regarding the productivity of domestic and industrial labour, which is part of an ongoing debate in the *New Left Review*.

10. Canada, Royal Commission on the Status of Women in Canada, *Report*, p. 34.

11. An alternative view is presented by Margrit Eichler, "The Industrialization of Housework."

12. Canada, Royal Commission on the Status of Women in Canada, *Report*, pp. 34-35.
13. Like the concept of poverty, the concept of necessity as it is used here does not imply absolute conditions and must be interpreted in historical and cultural terms.
14. Jenny Podoluk, *Incomes of Canadians*, p. 184.
15. How and why the capitalist system creates new needs, builds in obsolescence and increases consumer debt is explained by Paul A. Baran and Paul M. Sweezy in *Monopoly Capital*. It is also important to specify here the way in which the concept *economic necessity* is being used in this research. With reference to the principle of structural causality the concept of economic necessity must be understood as an explanatory principle at a broad structural level. It does not imply a cause-effect relationship at the individual level. In other words, the concept of economic necessity specifies a structural relationship which is not meant to be applied at the level of the individual (that is, to any given woman).
16. While the sample did not represent a cross section of divorced, widowed, and separated working women, for married women living with their husbands "the sample is fairly representative, and they make up 88% of the total" (Canada, Department of Labour, *A Survey of Married Women Working for Pay in Eight Canadian Cities*, p. 11).
17. Ibid., p. 42.
18. As the authors point out, the combined incomes of husbands and wives in the sample cannot be precisely compared with total income for Canadian families (ibid.).
19. Ibid., p. 48.
20. Podoluk, *Incomes of Canadians*, pp. 132-133.
21. Canada, Department of Labour, *Women at Work in Canada: 1964*, p. 6.
22. Leo A. Johnson, *Poverty in Wealth*, p. 4.
23. This part of the discussion is based on an important article by Hugh Armstrong and Patricia Armstrong, "The Segregated Participation of Women in the Canadian Labour Force, 1941-1971," pp. 370-384.
24. Ibid.
25. Ibid.
26. The family as a private unit of consumption is required in a capitalist society. Consequently "a residual portion of the [domestic] work that accomplishes this consumption is structurally necessary regardless of advances in household tech-

nology, child care services, etc." (Seccombe, "Domestic Labour — Reply to Critics," p. 92).

Chapter 9

1. See Patricia Connelly and Linda Christiansen-Ruffman, "Women's Problems," pp. 167-177.

Appendix A

1. Warren E. Kalbach and Wayne W. McVey, Jr., *The Demographic Basis of Canadian Society*, p. 4.
2. Noah M. Meltz, *Manpower in Canada, 1931-1961*.
3. For a discussion of the old and new occupational classifications see Canada, Statistics Canada, *The Labour Force,* August 1973.
4. Canada, Department of Labour, Women's Bureau, *Women in the Labour Force*; Canada, Department of Labour, *A Survey of Married Women Working for Pay in Eight Canadian Cities*; Canada, Department of Labour, *Occupational Histories of Married Women Working for Pay*; Canada, Royal Commission on the Status of Women in Canada, *Report*.

Bibliography

Abbott, Edith. *Women in Industry: A Study in American Economic History*. 1905. Reprint. New York: Arno Press, 1969.

Archibald, Kathleen. *Sex and the Public Service*. Ottawa: Queen's Printer, 1970.

Armstrong, Hugh, and Armstrong, Patricia. "The Segregated Participation of Women in the Canadian Labour Force, 1941-1971." *Canadian Review of Sociology and Anthropology* 12 (November 1975): 370-384.

Baran, Paul A., and Hobsbawm, Eric J. "The Method of Historical Materialism." In *The Capitalist System*, edited by Richard C. Edwards, Michael Reich, and G. E. Weisskopf, pp. 53-56. New Jersey: Prentice Hall, 1972.

Baran, Paul A., and Sweezy, Paul M. *Monopoly Capital: An Essay on the American Economic and Social Order*. New York: Monthly Review Press, 1966.

Benston, Margaret. "The Political Economy of Women's Liberation." *Monthly Review* 21 (September 1969): 13-27.

Boyd, Monica. "The Status of Immigrant Women in Canada." In *Women in Canada*, rev. ed., edited by Marylee Stephenson, pp. 228-244. Don Mills, Ontario: General Publishing Co., 1977.

Braverman, Harry. *Labor and Monopoly Capital*. New York: Monthly Review Press, 1974.

Canada, Department of Labour. *A Survey of Married Women Working for Pay in Eight Canadian Cities*. Ottawa: Queen's Printer, 1958.

——— . *Occupational Histories of Married Women Working for Pay*. Ottawa: Queen's Printer, 1959.

——— . *Women at Work in Canada: A Fact Book on the Female Labour Force, 1964*. Ottawa: Queen's Printer, 1965.

——— . *Women in the Labour Force: Facts and Figures*. Ottawa: Information Canada, 1975.

Canada, Dominion Bureau of Statistics. *Reserve of Labour Among*

Canadian Women. Statistics Canada no. 71-D-51. Ottawa, 1942.

Canada, Royal Commission of the Status of Women in Canada. *Report*. Ottawa: Information Canada, 1970.

Canada, Statistics Canada (formerly Dominion Bureau of Statistics). *Censuses of Canada, 1921, 1931, 1941, 1951, 1961, 1971*.Ottawa: Information Canada.

——— . "Comparison of the 1975 Labour Force Survey Estimates Derived from the Former and Revised Surveys." Mimeographed. Ottawa, 1976.

——— . "Conceptual, Definitional, and Methodological Change in the Labour Force Survey." Mimeographed. Ottawa, 1976.

Clark, Alice. *The Working Life of Women in the Seventeenth Century*. 1919. Reprint. New York: A.M. Kelley, 1968.

Coburn, Judi. "'I See and am Silent': A Short History of Nursing in Ontario." In *Women at Work: Ontario, 1850-1930*, edited by Janice Acton, Penny Goldsmith, and Bonnie Shepard, pp. 127-164. Toronto: Canadian Women's Educational Press, 1974.

Connelly, Patricia. "Women in Trade Unions." Working paper presented at the Conference on Blue Collar Workers, York University, Toronto, Ontario, May 1975. Mimeographed.

Connelly, Patricia, and Christiansen-Ruffman, Linda. "Women's Problems: Private Troubles or Public Issues." *Canadian Journal of Sociology* 2 (Spring 1977): 167-177.

Denton, Frank. *The Growth of Manpower in Canada*. Ottawa: Queen's Printer, 1970.

Eichler, Margrit. "The Industrialization of Housework." Paper presented at the National Council of Family Relations Meetings, October 1976. Mimeographed.

Gelber, Sylva, ed. "The Compensation of Women." In *Women's Bureau '74*, pp. 7-16. Ottawa: Information Canada, 1975.

——— . "The Economic and Academic Status of Women in Relation to Their Male Colleagues." In *Women's Bureau '74*, pp. 39-44. Ottawa: Information Canada, 1975.

——— . "Women's Responsibility in the Search for Equality of Rights." In *Women's Bureau '72*, pp. 21-28. Ottawa: Information Canada, 1973.

Geoffroy, Renée, and Sainte-Marie, Paule. *Attitudes of Union Workers to Women in Industry*. Ottawa: Information Canada, 1971.

Gordon, David M. *Theories of Poverty and Underemployment: Orthodox, Radical, and Dual Labor Market Perspectives*. Lexington, Mass.: Lexington Books, 1972.

Gunderson, Morley. "Work Patterns." In *Opportunity for Choice*, edited by Gail C.A. Cook, pp. 93-142. Ottawa: Statistics Canada in Association with the C.D. Howe Research Institute, 1976.

Hartmann, Heidi. "Capitalism, Patriarchy, and Job Segregation by Sex." *Signs: Journal of Women in Culture and Society* 1 (Spring 1976): 137-169.

Henry, Alice. *Women and the Labour Movement.* 1923. Reprint. New York: Arno Press, 1971.

Johnson, Leo A. "The Development of Class in Canada in the Twentieth Century." In *Capitalism and the National Question in Canada*, edited by Gary Teeple, pp. 141-183. Toronto: University of Toronto Press, 1972.

————. *Poverty in Wealth: The Capitalist Labour Market and Income Distribution in Canada.* Rev. ed. Toronto: New Hogtown Press, 1974.

————. "The Political Economy of Ontario Women in the Nineteenth Century." In *Women at Work: Ontario, 1850-1930*, edited by Janice Acton, Penny Goldsmith, and Bonnie Shepard, pp. 13-31. Toronto: Canadian Women's Educational Press, 1974.

Klein, Alice, and Roberts, Wayne. "Besieged Innocence: The 'Problem' and Problems of Working Women — Toronto, 1896-1914." In *Women at Work: Ontario, 1850-1930*, edited by Janice Acton, Penny Goldsmith, and Bonnie Shepard, pp. 211-260. Toronto: Canadian Women's Educational Press, 1974.

Kalbach, Warren E., and McVey, Wayne W., Jr. *The Demographic Basis of Canadian Society.* Toronto: McGraw-Hill, 1971.

Leslie, Genevieve. "Domestic Service in Canada, 1880-1920." In *Women at Work: Ontario, 1850-1930*, edited by Janice Acton, Penny Goldsmith, and Bonnie Shepard, pp. 71-126. Toronto: Canadian Women's Educational Press, 1974.

Lipton, Charles. *The Trade Union Movement of Canada, 1827-1959.* Toronto: NC Press, 1973.

Lowe, Graham. "Trends in the Development of Clerical Occupations in Canada, 1901-1931." Paper presented at the Annual Meeting of the Canadian Sociology and Anthropology Association, Fredericton, N.B., July 1977. Mimeographed.

MacLeod, Neil. "Female Earnings in Manufacturing: A Comparison with Male Earnings." In *Notes on Labour Statistics, 1971*, pp. 41-48. Ottawa: Information Canada, March 1972.

Madden, Janice. *The Economics of Sex Discrimination.* Toronto: D.C. Heath and Co., 1973.

Marsden, Lorna R. "Why Now? The Mirage of Equality." *Canadian Forum* 4 (September 1975): 12-17.

Marx, Karl. *Capital*. Vol. I. Edited by Friedrich Engels. New York: International Publishers, 1967.

——— . *A Contribution to the Critique of Political Economy*. New York: The International Library Publishing Co., 1904.

McDonald, Lynn. "Wages of Work: A Widening Gap between Women and Men." *Canadian Forum* 4 (April-May 1975): 4-7.

Meltz, Noah M. *Changes in the Occupational Composition of the Canadian Labour Force, 1931-1961*. Ottawa: Queen's Printer, 1965.

——— . *Manpower in Canada, 1931-1961: Historical Statistics of the Canadian Labour Force*. Ottawa: Queen's Printer, 1969.

Naylor, R.T. "The Rise and Fall of the Third Commercial Empire of the St. Lawrence." In *Capitalism and the National Question in Canada*, edited by Gary Teeple, pp. 1-41. Toronto: University of Toronto Press, 1972.

Ontario, Ministry of Community and Social Services, Provincial Benefits Branch and Income Security Secretariat. *It Pays to Work*. Toronto: 1976.

Oppenheimer, Valerie Kincade, *The Female Labor Force in the United States: Demographic and Economic Factors Governing its Growth and Changing Composition*. Population Monograph Series, no. 5. Berkeley, California: Institute of International Studies, 1970.

Ostry, Sylvia. *The Female Worker in Canada*. Ottawa: Queen's Printer, 1968.

Ostry, Sylvia, and Zaidi, Mahmood A. *Labour Economics in Canada*. Toronto: Macmillan Co. of Canada, 1972.

Pentland, H.C. "The Development of a Capitalistic Labour Market in Canada." *Canadian Journal of Economics and Political Science* 25 (November 1959): 450-461.

Pinchbeck, Ivy. *Women Workers and the Industrial Revolution, 1750-1850*. London: George Routledge and Sons, 1930.

Podoluk, Jenny. *Incomes of Canadians*. Ottawa: Queen's Printer, 1968.

Ramkhalawansingh, Ceta. "Women During the Great War." In *Women at Work: Ontario, 1850-1930*, edited by Janice Acton, Penny Goldsmith, and Bonnie Shepard, pp. 261-308. Toronto: Canadian Women's Educational Press, 1974.

Rotenberg, Lori. "The Wayward Worker: Toronto's Prostitute at the Turn of the Century." In *Women at Work: Ontario, 1850-1930*, edited by Janice Acton, Penny Goldsmith, and Bonnie Shepard, pp. 33-70. Toronto: Canadian Women's Educational Press, 1974.

Ryerson, Stanley. *Unequal Union*. Toronto: Progress Books, 1968.

Seccombe, Wally. "Domestic Labour — Reply to Critics." *New Left*

Review 94 (November-December 1975): 85-96.

Smith, Dorothy, and Marsden, Lorna. "Equal Pay for Work of Equal Value." Paper presented at the joint session of the Canadian Political Science Association and Canadian Sociology and Anthrolology Association on Sex, Work and Equal Pay, Québec City, Québec, May, 1976. Mimeographed.

Spencer, Byron, and Featherstone, Dennis. *Married Female Labour Force Participation: A Micro Study.* Ottawa: Dominion Bureau of Statistics, 1970.

Sweezy, Paul M. *The Theory of Capitalist Development: Principles of Marxian Political Economy.* New York: Monthly Review Press, 1942.

Veltmeyer, Henry. "Marx's Two Methods of Social Analysis." *Sociological Inquiry*, in press.

"The Methodology of Dependency Analysis: A Strategy for Research on Regional Underdevelopment." *Canadian Journal of Political and Social Theory*, in press.

Zaretsky, Eli. "Capitalism, the Family and Personal Life." *Socialist Revolution* 3, nos. 13, 14 (1973).